AI Risk Management for Financial Institutions

Building Defensible Governance for Vendor-Driven AI

Barry A. Salas

Apress®

AI Risk Management for Financial Institutions: Building Defensible Governance for Vendor-Driven AI

Barry A. Salas
Vancouver, WA, USA

ISBN-13 (pbk): 979-8-8688-3352-6 ISBN-13 (electronic): 979-8-8688-3353-3
https://doi.org/10.1007/979-8-8688-3353-3

Managing Director, Apress Media LLC: Welmoed Spahr
Acquisitions Editor: Celestin Suresh John
Editorial Assistant: Gryffin Winkler

Cover designed by eStudioCalamar

Distributed to the book trade worldwide by Springer Science+Business Media New York, 1 New York Plaza, New York, NY 10004. Phone 1-800-SPRINGER, fax (201) 348-4505, e-mail orders-ny@springer-sbm.com, or visit www.springeronline.com. Apress Media, LLC is a Delaware LLC and the sole member (owner) is Springer Science + Business Media Finance Inc (SSBM Finance Inc). SSBM Finance Inc is a **Delaware** corporation.

For information on translations, please e-mail booktranslations@springernature.com; for reprint, paperback, or audio rights, please e-mail bookpermissions@springernature.com.

Apress titles may be purchased in bulk for academic, corporate, or promotional use. eBook versions and licenses are also available for most titles. For more information, reference our Print and eBook Bulk Sales web page at http://www.apress.com/bulk-sales.

Any source code or other supplementary material referenced by the author in this book is available to readers on GitHub. For more detailed information, please visit https://www.apress.com/gp/services/source-code.

If disposing of this product, please recycle the paper

To my wife and daughter, who support me in everything I do, including my shenanigans.

Table of Contents

About the Author

Barry A. Salas is an Information Security Program Manager with deep expertise in governance, risk management, and regulatory defensibility within financial institutions. He holds an MS in Information Systems from the University of Texas at Arlington. He has designed and implemented AI governance and security programs aligned with NCUA, FFIEC, GLBA, and NIST frameworks, with a strong focus on practical execution. Barry's work emphasizes building defensible, regulator-ready solutions tailored for resource-constrained environments, helping institutions manage emerging AI risks with clarity and confidence. He is based in Vancouver, WA, USA.

About the Technical Reviewer

Aritra is a hands-on Digital FinTech Servant Leader with significant experience in financial modeling, capital markets, and financial risk management functionalities. Aritra has a keen interest in AI and has been executing projects with the application of machine learning in financial modeling.

Aritra is a versatile hands-on leader with a quantitative bent of mind, skilled in running complex projects and developing automation initiatives to propel growth and add bottom-line value while managing risk. Additionally, he is passionate about community building and knowledge sharing and actively contributes to the tech ecosystem by reviewing technical books, publishing whitepapers, authoring articles, speaking at AI conferences, and serving as judge on expert industry panels.

Acknowledgments

Thank you to the team at Apress for taking a chance on this book and for the patience shown along the way from proposal to final draft. Turning a stack of ideas into something that actually holds together took real editorial work, and I'm grateful for it.

I'm indebted to the credit union I'm currently working for; they allowed me the space to create a security program from the beginning and learn more through that experience than any school could have taught me. The problems that show up in these pages are ones I've worked through firsthand, not ones I've read about.

Before that, First Hawaiian Bank gave me my first genuine look at how financial institutions actually operate and how much friction exists between what technology promises and what a regulated, risk-averse industry can absorb. My current perspective on this field stems from that early exposure.

And to my years in military service, thank you for teaching me how to approach a problem: assess first, act deliberately, and don't mistake motion for progress. This book exhibits that mindset more than any single chapter acknowledges.

Introduction

Building an AI governance program at a credit union is not work that comes with a roadmap. When AI capabilities began appearing across my institution, embedded in vendor platforms, adopted informally by staff, arriving through routine software updates, I searched for practical guidance written for institutions like mine: small teams, constrained resources, and a regulatory environment that was asking increasingly specific questions we had no formal framework to answer. I found frameworks designed for enterprise AI development teams and academic analyses of risks we were not yet equipped to manage. What I did not find was a practitioner's guide for the information security and risk professional at a community financial institution who needs to build a defensible AI governance program, largely from scratch, while managing a full portfolio of other responsibilities. So, I wrote one.

While this book focuses on credit unions, the governance frameworks and methodology it presents apply broadly to any community financial institution managing AI risk under resource constraints. The credit union context is the one I know from direct program experience, and it is where I have observed the most acute governance gaps. Every scenario, framework, and practical guidance in these pages is drawn from that work. My gratitude goes to the team and colleagues who were part of building it.

Let's discuss this book's process. The book contains five parts. Part I establishes the context: how AI arrived in credit union environments, how to think about AI risk, and what the regulatory landscape requires. Part II covers preparation: how to evaluate AI before deployment, how to conduct risk assessments, and how to apply the AI Vendor Risk Evaluation Model to third-party relationships. Part III addresses governing AI that is already in operation: building and maintaining the inventory, managing shadow AI, governing data flows, understanding security risks, and establishing the monitoring program. Part IV builds the formal governance infrastructure: the framework, the committee, the control model, and incident response. Part V addresses strategic oversight and the forward horizon: board engagement, responsible AI as a cooperative value, and what the future of AI governance in financial services is likely to require.

Each chapter follows a consistent structure: an opening scenario grounded in the kinds of situations credit union practitioners encounter, followed by the risk problem, the credit union–specific context, the governance framework, implementation steps, important points, and questions for leadership. The appendix provides ten working templates that can be adapted and deployed immediately.

Four proprietary frameworks run through the book as its intellectual spine: the AI Governance Pyramid, the AI Risk Classification Model, the AI Vendor Risk Evaluation Model, and the AI Governance Committee Structure. These frameworks emerged from the work of building a real program at a real institution. They are not theoretical constructs; they are tools that were tested against actual governance challenges and refined in response to what those challenges revealed.

This book targets financial institutions that primarily consume AI rather than develop it. The governance challenges it addresses, including vendor-embedded AI, shadow AI, model opacity, limited resources, and regulatory uncertainty, are those faced by institutions that manage AI systems they did not build, deployed by vendors whose model documentation ranges from excellent to nearly nonexistent, and staffed by teams that do not include dedicated AI specialists. If you are reading this as someone building your own models or managing an enterprise AI development program, there are better resources written specifically for your context. If you are reading this as someone responsible for governing

AI at a community financial institution where the governance program largely needs to be built by one or two people who have a dozen other responsibilities, this book is for you.

I hope that when you finish reading it, the program ahead of you feels achievable rather than overwhelming. It is achievable. The practitioners working in financial institutions today, building security programs, managing vendor portfolios, navigating examinations, and protecting members, already have every capability needed to govern AI well. What most are missing is a framework, a methodology, and guidance from someone who has done the work. This book is my attempt to provide all three.

PART I

The AI Reality in Credit Unions

Chapters 1–3 establish the foundation: how AI arrived in credit union environments without formal governance, what that means for institutional risk, and what the regulatory landscape currently requires.

CHAPTER 1

The Quiet Arrival of AI in Financial Institutions

Opening Scenario

It is a Tuesday morning at a mid-sized credit union. The VP of Lending is reviewing the latest loan approval queue when she notices something odd. Decisions that used to take hours are coming back in minutes. She mentions it to her team lead, who shrugs and says the core system vendor pushed an update last quarter. Nobody thought much of it.

Downstairs, in the IT department, the security program manager is reviewing a vendor renewal when he spots a line item buried in the updated terms of service: "Services may use machine learning and AI-assisted analytics to improve performance and accuracy." He read it twice. Then he opens the vendor's product page. Sure enough, listed under a "What's New" tab, the fraud detection module now includes an" AI-powered behavioral scoring engine."

Nobody approved it. Nobody assessed it. It arrived quietly, embedded in a routine software update, and it had been making recommendations about member accounts for ninety days.

B. A. Salas, *AI Risk Management for Financial Institutions*,
https://doi.org/10.1007/979-8-8688-3353-3_1

Meanwhile, in the marketing department, three staff members have been using a popular generative AI tool to draft member newsletters and promotional email campaigns. They found it six months ago, started using it informally, and it quickly became part of their daily workflow. None of them thought to ask IT or security. It was free; it worked well, and it saved hours each week. The fact that they were occasionally pasting member demographic language into the prompts to personalize content—that never came up in conversation.

On the operations side, a business analyst recently discovered that the ticketing platform the team had been using for two years had quietly introduced an AI triage feature that was now automatically categorizing and routing member service requests. Default had enabled the feature in the latest platform update. Nobody had turned it on. Nobody had turned it off. It had simply been running.

Ninety days. The rough equivalent of two board meetings, one vendor renewal nobody had gotten around to, and approximately four hundred other priorities.

By the time the Information Security Program Manager connected these dots, the credit union had AI operating in four distinct areas of the business: lending, fraud, marketing, and operations, none of them formally inventoried, none of them risk-assessed, and none of them reviewed by compliance or legal.

This is not an unusual story. It is the typical one.

The Risk Problem

Artificial intelligence did not arrive at most financial institutions through a formal procurement process, the kind with a risk assessment, vendor due diligence review, and board awareness. It arrived through product updates, staff convenience, and vendor enthusiasm. It arrived quietly, and many times, it is still operating quietly today.

The core risk problem is not that AI is inherently dangerous. The risk is that institutions have assumed passive exposure when they are actually in active use. A vendor that embeds a machine learning model into its platform and enables it by default has introduced an AI system into your environment—regardless of whether your team made a deliberate decision to use it. A staff member who pastes member account details into a generative AI prompt to draft a letter has introduced an AI data-handling event, regardless of whether IT knows it is happening.

That gap between assumed and actual AI exposure is where regulatory, reputational, and operational risk lives.

For credit unions specifically, the challenge is compounded by resource constraints. Most credit unions do not have dedicated AI risk teams, enterprise AI architects, or standing governance committees reviewing model deployments. The Chief Information Security Officer, the Information Security Program Manager, or the Chief Risk Officer is often the person who must figure this out, while simultaneously managing endpoint security, incident response, compliance audits, and vendor renewals. Developing AI governance programs on the scale of Google's is never expected of small institutions. The expectation is that they will build defensible, proportionate programs that reflect the actual risks in their environment.

The quiet arrival of AI creates a governance deficit that compounds. Unreviewed systems add to the inventory gap. Each unassessed model adds to the risk exposure. Each month that passes without a formal program makes the remediation effort larger. The good news is that the path forward is not complicated; however, it requires clarity, structure, and the willingness to begin.

Why It Matters to Credit Unions

Credit unions operate under a specific regulatory environment. National Credit Union Administration (NCUA) examiners are increasingly asking about AI governance during safety and soundness examinations—a shift reflected in published NCUA supervisory priorities citing technology risk and third-party AI relationships and illustrated in the examination scenario that opens Chapter 3. The Federal Financial Institutions Examination Council (FFIEC) has signaled clear expectations around model risk management that extend to AI and machine learning systems. Gramm-Leach-Bliley Act (GLBA) Safeguards Rule obligations around data protection apply regardless of whether member data is being processed by a human analyst or an automated model.

Beyond regulatory exposure, there is a member trust dimension that is unique to the credit union model. Credit unions are not banks. Credit unions build relationships with members on a cooperative foundation, and the institution exists to serve its members, not to profit from them. When an AI system makes a lending decision, generates a fraud flag, or shapes a product recommendation based on member data, that action carries the implicit weight of that trust relationship.

A member who is incorrectly flagged for fraud by an opaque AI model has experienced harm that no automated system can fully remediate. A member who receives a loan denial driven by a scoring algorithm that the institution cannot explain has encountered a failure that compliance language alone cannot resolve. These are not hypothetical risks. They are the predictable outcomes of deploying AI systems without governance.

The credit union movement has long distinguished itself through transparency, accessibility, and genuine member-first service. AI governance is not a departure from those values; it is their extension into a new operational environment. Getting it right is both a regulatory obligation and a reflection of institutional character.

Governance and Risk Considerations

Most credit unions are already using AI. The more important question is whether anyone in the institution recognizes how it operates, and whether anyone is overseeing it.

Answering that question requires three foundational capabilities: visibility, accountability, and defensibility.

Visibility means knowing where AI exists in vendor platforms, internal tools, staff-adopted applications, and any embedded functionality that uses machine learning or automated decision-making. Without a basic AI inventory, governance is impossible.

Accountability means knowing who owns AI risk. AI governance is not an IT problem. It is not a security problem. It is an enterprise risk problem that requires executive visibility, board awareness, and cross-functional ownership. When AI risk has no named owner, it belongs to everyone in theory and no one in practice.

Defensibility means having documentation that can withstand examiner scrutiny: policies that address AI use, risk assessments for systems in use, vendor due diligence that includes AI-specific questions, and evidence that leadership has engaged with the topic. Defensibility does not require perfection. It requires a demonstrable good-faith program.

Framework Reference: AI Governance Pyramid The AI Governance Pyramid, introduced in Chapter 2, provides the structural model for this program.

It establishes five layers of governance: from the AI systems themselves at the foundation through Operational Controls, Risk Management, Governance Program, and Strategic Oversight at the top.

Each chapter in this book builds upward through that model.

Before that structure can be built, leadership must accept a foundational premise: AI governance cannot live entirely in the IT department. The decisions that AI systems make about loans, about fraud, about member communications are business decisions with regulatory consequences. Governance must follow the risk, and the risk lives across the enterprise.

Implementation Steps

People can achieve these initial steps before a formal AI governance program is in place.

These initial steps create the foundation for everything else.

1. Conduct an initial AI exposure survey. Ask department heads, IT, and key business unit leads to identify any tools, vendor platforms, or staff-adopted applications that use AI or machine learning. A simple questionnaire is sufficient at this stage.
2. Create a preliminary AI inventory, even if informal. For each identified system, document the system name, vendor, primary use case, whether it touches member data, and who is currently responsible for it.
3. Flag any AI-enabled vendor platforms for review at their next renewal cycle. Ensure that AI usage, data handling, and model transparency are addressed as part of vendor due diligence going forward.

4. Brief executive leadership on the concept of shadow AI, staff-adopted tools operating outside IT and security visibility. This briefing does not need to be alarmist. It needs to create an awareness that the issue exists and that a response is being developed.

5. Designate a provisional owner for AI governance activities. Until a formal committee is established, assign a named individual, likely the Information Security Program Manager, the Chief Risk Officer, or the Chief Information Officer, to coordinate AI governance actions and serve as the point of contact for examiner questions.

Important Points

- AI has arrived in most credit unions through passive channels: vendor updates and staff adoption, rather than formal procurement decisions.
- The gap between assumed and actual AI exposure is the primary governance risk at this stage of institutional maturity.
- Regulatory expectations around AI are increasing. NCUA, FFIEC, and GLBA obligations apply to AI systems, whether or not the institution has a formal AI program.
- Member trust is a governance asset unique to the credit union model; one that AI deployments can erode if oversight is absent.
- The first governance action is visibility. You cannot assess, manage, or defend what you have not identified.

Questions for Leadership

1. Do we know every place in our organization where AI is currently being used, including AI embedded in vendor platforms?
2. Has any department adopted AI tools informally, outside the IT procurement and security review process?
3. Do our existing vendor contracts address AI usage, data handling, and model transparency?
4. Who in our organization currently owns AI risk, and do they have the visibility and authority to act on it?
5. If an NCUA examiner asked us today to describe our AI governance program, what would we say—and would that answer be adequate?

Further Reading

- NIST AI Risk Management Framework (AI RMF 1.0)—National Institute of Standards and Technology.
- FFIEC IT Examination Handbook, Management Booklet—Federal Financial Institutions Examination Council.
- NCUA Letter to Credit Unions on Third-Party Relationships—National Credit Union Administration.
- GLBA Safeguards Rule (16 CFR Part 314)—Federal Trade Commission.
- Interagency Guidance on Model Risk Management (SR 11-7)—Federal Reserve/OCC.

CHAPTER 2

Understanding AI Risk in Financial Institutions

Opening Scenario

The Information Security Program Manager had just returned from an industry conference where AI governance dominated the agenda. Every session referenced large financial institutions: enterprise banks with AI ethics boards, dedicated model risk management teams, and multimillion-dollar governance infrastructure. On the flight home, he opened his laptop and stared at his own environment: a forty-person IT department, a two-person security team, and a vendor portfolio that had quietly accumulated AI capabilities across lending, fraud, and member services.

The conference was useful but disorienting. The frameworks presented were real: NIST AI Risk Management Framework (AI RMF), ISO/IEC 42001:2030, internal model validation pipelines, but they were built for organizations ten times his size. When he tried to mentally map them to his credit union, the fit was poor. His institution did not deploy its own models. It consumed vendor AI. It did not have a model validation team. It had a security program manager and a Risk Committee that met quarterly.

B. A. Salas, *AI Risk Management for Financial Institutions*,
https://doi.org/10.1007/979-8-8688-3353-3_2

What he needed was a way to think about AI risk that matched his actual operating environment, a mental model that was proportionate, practical, and defensible. Not a framework built for enterprise AI development teams, but a governance structure built for institutions that are primarily AI consumers, not AI builders.

He started sketching on a notepad. At the bottom, the AI systems themselves: the models, the vendor tools, and the embedded capabilities he was still discovering. Above that are the operational controls: security, data governance, and vendor oversight. Then risk management: assessments, the classification decisions, and ongoing monitoring. Then the governance program: policies, accountability, committees. And at the top, the piece that held it all together and gave it institutional authority: strategic oversight from leadership and the board.

Five layers. A pyramid. Though not every layer was fully built, a clear picture of a complete program existed, revealing its gaps. He drew an arrow pointing to the space between the bottom two layers and wrote a single word: "Start here."

The Risk Problem

The fundamental challenge with AI risk is that it does not fit neatly into existing risk categories. It is not purely operational risk, although it has operational dimensions. It is not purely a technology risk, though it lives inside technology systems. It is not purely compliance risk, though regulatory consequences follow when it goes wrong. AI risk is cross-cutting; it touches every risk domain the institution manages, and it requires an equally broad governance response.

For credit unions operating primarily as AI consumers rather than AI developers, the risk profile is distinct from what most AI governance literature describes. The institution is not building models or training algorithms. It is deploying vendor AI, relying on embedded AI in core systems and ancillary platforms, and managing the growing informal adoption of generative AI tools by staff.

Five principal risk categories define the AI consumer risk profile:

- **Opacity risk**: The institution cannot explain how a vendor AI model reaches its conclusions, which creates member-facing and regulatory exposure when decisions are challenged.
- **Data exposure risk**: AI systems, particularly generative AI tools, may ingest, transmit, or keep member data in ways that violate GLBA obligations or vendor contractual terms.
- **Dependency risk**: Increasing reliance on AI-powered vendor functions creates operational vulnerability if those systems fail, change behavior, or are discontinued.
- **Governance gap risk**: The absence of formal AI oversight means that risk accumulates faster than it is identified, and the institution cannot demonstrate a defensible program to examiners.
- **Embedded AI drift risk**: Vendor AI systems evolve continuously through updates and model retraining, meaning a system assessed as low risk today may behave differently in twelve months, triggering no formal review.

Understanding AI risk begins with accepting that the risk is dynamic. Unlike static controls or a policy that, once implemented, remains stable, AI systems change over time. Governance must account for that variability through monitoring, periodic reassessment, and vendor accountability mechanisms.

Why It Matters to Credit Unions

The size and complexity of a credit union do not reduce its regulatory exposure for AI risk; it reduces its capacity to manage that risk without a structured approach. A community bank with a hundred-person compliance department and a $5 billion AI governance program has more resources. It does not have fewer obligations.

NCUA's examination focuses on third-party relationships, model risk management, and data governance, all of which intersect directly with AI. An institution that cannot inventory its AI systems, explain how vendor AI models function, or show board-level awareness of AI risk is exposed, not because it made a bad technology decision but because it made no governance decision at all.

The proportionality principle that runs through most financial services regulation applies here as well. Examiners do not expect a ten-branch credit union to operate the same AI governance infrastructure as the top twenty banks. They expect a program that is commensurate with the institution's size, complexity, and risk profile. That standard is achievable. What is not achievable is the absence of a program entirely.

Governance and Risk Considerations

The AI Governance Pyramid is the foundational model for this book. It provides the structural framework that organizes every chapter that follows. Understanding the pyramid, what each layer represents, what it requires, and how the layers relate to one another, is an essential context for everything else.

The Five Layers of the AI Governance Pyramid

Figure 2-1. *The AI Governance Pyramid—five layers of governance for credit union AI programs*

Layer 1—AI Systems: Models, Vendor AI, Embedded AI Capabilities

Layer 1: AI Systems

The foundation of the pyramid is the AI systems themselves; every model, vendor tool, embedded capability, and staff-adopted application that uses artificial intelligence or machine learning in any form. This is where the risk originates. Governance cannot function without first knowing what it governs.

For most credit unions, this layer is not fully visible at the outset. AI systems have arrived through vendor updates, default-enabled features, and informal staff adoption. The first task of governance is to make this layer legible; to build and maintain an inventory of AI systems that is accurate, current, and actionable.

Layer 2: Operational Controls

The second layer encompasses the controls that govern how AI systems behave within the operational environment: security controls that protect AI systems and the data they process, data governance mechanisms that define how member information flows into and out of AI systems, and vendor oversight processes that hold third-party AI providers accountable to contractual and regulatory standards.

Operational controls are where AI governance intersects most directly with existing security and risk programs. Many institutions already have frameworks in this space: vendor management programs, data classification policies, and security control libraries. The work at this layer is often an extension rather than creation: adapting existing controls to account for AI-specific risk vectors.

Layer 3: AI Risk Management

The third layer is the risk management function: the processes by which AI systems are assessed, classified by risk level, and monitored over time. This layer translates the inventory and controls below it into a risk posture that leadership can understand and act on. It answers the question: Of everything we know about our AI systems and the controls we have around them, what is our actual risk exposure, and is it acceptable?

Risk management at this level is not a one-time exercise. AI systems change. Vendor models are retrained. New capabilities are added. Staff adoption evolves. The risk management function must be periodic, structured, and tied to a classification model that allows the institution to prioritize its oversight effort proportionately.

Layer 4: AI Governance Program

The fourth layer is the formal governance infrastructure: the policies that define acceptable AI use, the accountability structures that assign ownership for AI risk, and the governance committees that provide institutional oversight. This layer transforms individual risk management activities into a coherent, documented program that the institution can stand behind in an examination, a board meeting, or a member inquiry.

Without this layer, the work done in Layers 1 through 3 exists as disconnected activity rather than a defensible program. Governance program infrastructure connects the operational reality of AI in the environment to the institutional accountability structures above it.

Layer 5: Strategic Oversight

The apex of the pyramid is strategic oversight: the engagement of board governance and executive leadership in AI risk. This layer does not require board members to understand machine learning models. It requires that leadership receive meaningful information about AI risks, ask informed questions, and exercise appropriate oversight of the institution's AI governance program.

Strategic oversight transforms a technical risk management function into an institutional commitment. It is also what examiners look for when they assess whether an institution takes AI governance seriously. Board engagement does not have to be deep to be defensible. It has to be genuine, documented, and connected to the risk information flowing up from the layers below.

How to Use This Model The AI Governance Pyramid is referenced throughout this book as a navigation tool.

Part II (Chapters 4–6) builds Layer 1 and Layer 2.

Part III (Chapters 7–11) deepens Layer 2 and builds Layer 3.

Part IV (Chapters 12–15) constructs Layer 4 and connects it to Layer 3.

Part V (Chapters 16–18) addresses Layer 5 and the strategic horizon.

Each chapter will show which layer it primarily addresses.

Implementation Steps

1. Use the pyramid as a self-assessment tool. For each layer, ask: Does our institution have anything here? Document what exists, what is partial, and what is absent. This gap map becomes the first input to your AI governance roadmap.

2. Prioritize Layer 1 before everything else. Governance cannot function without visibility into the AI systems it governs. If your AI inventory is incomplete, make completing it the first program objective.

3. Identify which existing programs can extend into Layer 2. Vendor management, data governance, and security controls likely already exist in some form. Assess whether they address AI-specific risk, and document the gaps.

4. Do not build all five layers simultaneously. The pyramid is a target state, not a day-one requirement. Build upward in sequence. A strong Layer 1 and Layer 2 with a provisional Layer 3 is a more defensible program than five partially built layers with no coherent foundation.
5. Present the pyramid to executive leadership as a program roadmap. The visual model communicates the structure and the gaps without requiring technical depth from the audience. Use it to frame the governance conversation with leadership early.

Important Points

- AI risk is cross-cutting—it does not fit neatly into a single risk category and requires a governance response that spans operations, technology, compliance, and strategy.
- Credit unions operating as AI consumers face a distinct risk profile centered on opacity, data exposure, operational dependency, governance gaps, and AI system drift.
- The AI Governance Pyramid provides the structural framework for this book and for building a proportionate, defensible AI governance program.
- The five layers, AI Systems, Operational Controls, Risk Management, Governance Program, and Strategic Oversight, must be built in sequence. Visibility precedes control. Control precedes risk management. Risk management precedes a governance program. Governance programs are preceded by strategic oversight.

- Proportionality is the operative standard. The program must be commensurate with the institution's size, complexity, and actual AI risk exposure. It does not need to be perfect. It needs to be defensible.

Questions for Leadership

1. If we mapped our current AI activities against the five-layer pyramid, which layers are represented and which are absent?
2. Do we have documented visibility into all AI systems operating in our environment, including vendor-embedded AI?
3. Are our existing vendor management, data governance, and security programs explicitly addressing AI-specific risks?
4. Who currently owns AI risk in our institution, and is that ownership reflected in our governance structure?
5. Has the board received a briefing on AI risk that was specific enough to support informed oversight?

Further Reading

- NIST AI Risk Management Framework (AI RMF 1.0), GOVERN Function—National Institute of Standards and Technology

- FFIEC IT Examination Handbook, Audit Booklet—Federal Financial Institutions Examination Council
- SR 11-7: Guidance on Model Risk Management—Federal Reserve Board/OCC
- NCUA Supervisory Priorities, AI and Technology Risk—National Credit Union Administration
- ISO/IEC 42001:2023—Artificial Intelligence Management System Standard

CHAPTER 3

Regulatory Expectations and AI Governance

Opening Scenario

The NCUA examination had been scheduled for six weeks. The same Information Security Program Manager who had spent the prior months mapping the institution's AI exposure and sketching the outlines of a governance framework had spent those weeks preparing documentation, pulling evidence, and making sure the security program artifacts were organized and defensible. He felt reasonably confident going in.

The examiner arrived on a Monday morning and, after the usual opening meeting with the CEO and CFO, asked to spend time with the ISPM and the Chief Risk Officer (CRO). The first hour covered the expected territory: information security programs, incident response, and vendor management. Then the examiner opened a new line of questioning.

"Can you walk me through how your institution is managing AI risk?" she asked.

The ISPM had expected the question. What he had not expected was its scope. The examiner was not asking about a specific system or a specific vendor. She was asking about the institution's approach: its governance

B. A. Salas, *AI Risk Management for Financial Institutions*,
https://doi.org/10.1007/979-8-8688-3353-3_3

posture, its risk assessment methodology, and its board-level awareness. She referenced SR 11-7, the interagency model risk management guidance. She asked whether the institution had an AI inventory. She asked who owned AI-related decisions. She asked whether the board had received any AI risk briefings in the past twelve months.

The ISPM answered each question as honestly as he could. Some answers were strong. Several were not. The examiner's intent became clear by the conversation's conclusion: not a technology audit, but a governance review. The question was not whether the credit union had deployed AI responsibly. The question was whether it had a structure in place to ensure responsible deployment.

The examination finding that followed was not a formal violation. It was a matter requiring attention: the institution should develop a documented AI governance framework commensurate with its AI risk exposure. Remediation was expected within ninety days.

The ISPM left the closing meeting with a clear understanding of something he had suspected for months: regulatory expectations for AI were no longer hypothetical. They were present; they were documented, and they were showing up in examinations.

The Risk Problem

The regulatory landscape for AI in financial services is not static, and it is not simple. There is no single AI regulation that applies uniformly to credit unions. Instead, AI governance obligations are distributed across multiple existing frameworks: model risk management guidance, third-party relationship standards, data protection requirements, and consumer protection obligations. All of which apply to AI systems, whether or not they mention AI by name.

This is both a challenge and an opportunity. The challenge is that there is no single compliance checklist an institution can complete and call the matter resolved. The opportunity is that credit unions, which already have mature programs in vendor management, data governance, information security, and risk assessment, have much of the regulatory foundation already in place. This work is an extension, and the documentation is not constructed from scratch.

The regulatory risk for credit unions that ignore AI governance is not abstract. Examiners are increasingly trained to ask about AI. Interagency guidance is expanding. State-level regulations are emerging. Institutions that cannot show a proportionate, good-faith AI governance program are exposed to examination findings, matters requiring attention, and, in cases of member harm or enforcement action. The standard is not perfection. It is defensibility.

Why It Matters to Credit Unions

Credit unions are subject to a regulatory environment that is specific to their charter type and supervisory structure. NCUA is the primary federal regulator for federally chartered credit unions and the insurer of member deposits for federally insured state-chartered credit unions. State-chartered credit unions also operate under state regulatory requirements that may supplement or exceed federal standards.

NCUA has signaled clearly that AI governance is within the scope of its supervisory interests. Its supervisory priorities have referenced technology risk, third-party relationships, and model risk management in terms that encompass AI. NCUA examiners are not currently applying a formal AI-specific examination module at most institutions, but they are applying existing examination frameworks to AI activities, and those frameworks have real expectations.

For credit unions, the stakes of regulatory non-compliance are institutional in a way that differs from banks. A significant examination finding or enforcement action affects the institution's ability to serve its members, maintain its community standing, and attract the volunteer board leadership the cooperative model depends on. Regulatory defensibility is not just a compliance obligation; it is an institutional survival concern.

Governance and Risk Considerations

Understanding the regulatory landscape for AI requires mapping the existing frameworks that apply and identifying where they intersect with AI governance obligations. The following frameworks are the primary regulatory touchpoints for credit union AI governance.

SR 11-7: Model Risk Management

Supervisory Guidance on Model Risk Management, issued jointly by the Federal Reserve Board and the OCC in 2011, remains the most directly applicable regulatory framework for AI governance in financial services. Although it predates modern AI, SR 11-7 applies to any quantitative model used in decision-making—a definition that encompasses machine learning models, AI-powered scoring systems, and automated decision tools.

SR 11-7 establishes expectations for model development, validation, and ongoing monitoring. For credit unions consuming vendor AI rather than building their own models, the relevant obligations center on vendor-side validation documentation, understanding model assumptions and limitations, and maintaining the ability to challenge model outputs. An institution that deploys a vendor AI lending model without understanding how it works, what data it uses, or how it has been validated is operating outside the spirit of this guidance—and increasingly, outside examiner expectations.

FFIEC IT Examination Handbook

The FFIEC IT Examination Handbook provides the examination framework used by federal financial institution regulators, including the NCUA. Several booklets within the handbook are directly relevant to AI governance: the Management Booklet addresses governance and oversight structures; the Third-Party Relationships Booklet addresses vendor risk management obligations that extend to AI-enabled vendors; the Audit Booklet addresses independent review of technology risk; and the Development and Acquisition Booklet addresses technology procurement and change management processes that apply when AI capabilities are added to existing systems.

The FFIEC handbook does not use the term "AI governance" extensively, but its frameworks apply to AI activities comprehensively. Institutions that have built their existing technology governance programs against the FFIEC handbook are well-positioned to extend those programs to cover AI—the conceptual infrastructure is already in place.

GLBA Safeguards Rule

The Gramm-Leach-Bliley Act Safeguards Rule, administered by the FTC and applicable to financial institutions, including credit unions, establishes requirements for protecting customer financial information. The 2021 amendments to the Safeguards Rule strengthened its requirements and added specificity around encryption, access controls, and incident response.

AI systems intersect with GLBA obligations at multiple points. Generative AI tools that ingest member data trigger data protection obligations regardless of whether they are formally procurement-approved. Vendor AI systems that the institution's information security program and vendor oversight processes must cover process member financial information. AI-related data incidents—unauthorized disclosure of member data through an AI tool—trigger GLBA notification requirements. The Safeguards Rule does not carve out AI from its scope. AI is simply another way that member data can be processed, and its protection requirements apply.

Consumer Protection and Fair Lending Obligations

AI systems used in lending, marketing, or member-facing decision-making create consumer protection exposure that extends beyond information security. The Equal Credit Opportunity Act, the Fair Housing Act, and the Consumer Financial Protection Bureau's unfair, deceptive, or abusive acts or practices (UDAAP) standards all apply to AI-driven decisions that affect members.

Algorithmic bias—the risk that an AI model produces systematically different outcomes for members based on protected class characteristics, even without explicit discriminatory intent—is a live regulatory concern. Credit unions using vendor AI in lending or account management must understand whether their vendors have tested for disparate impact and must maintain documentation of that inquiry. The institution cannot disclaim responsibility for discriminatory outcomes by attributing them to vendor technology.

Emerging AI-Specific Guidance

In 2023, the federal financial regulators—the OCC, Federal Reserve, FDIC, NCUA, and CFPB—issued a joint Request for Information on financial institutions' use of AI, signaling coordinated regulatory attention to the topic. While formal AI-specific rule-making has been deliberate rather than rapid, the direction of travel is clear: expectations will become more explicit over time, and institutions that build governance programs now will be well-positioned for whatever specific requirements emerge.

The NIST AI Risk Management Framework, while not a regulatory requirement for credit unions, has been referenced by multiple regulatory bodies as a sound voluntary framework for AI governance. Institutions that align their programs to the NIST AI RMF—its four functions of GOVERN, MAP, MEASURE, and MANAGE—are building on a foundation that regulators have explicitly endorsed. Chapter 4 translates these regulatory expectations into the practical pre-deployment evaluation framework that credit unions can apply immediately.

Regulatory Touchpoint Summary SR 11-7—Model risk management; applies to AI models used in decision-making.

FFIEC IT Handbook—Technology governance, vendor management, audit; applies broadly.

GLBA Safeguards Rule—Member data protection; applies to all AI data handling.

ECOA/FHA/UDAAP—Fair lending and consumer protection; applies to AI decisions.

NIST AI RMF—Voluntary framework; referenced and endorsed by regulators.

NCUA Supervisory Priorities—Evolving; AI and technology risk explicitly included.

Implementation Steps

1. Map your AI inventory against the regulatory frameworks above. For each identified AI system, note which frameworks apply based on what the system does and what data it touches. A lending

AI triggers SR 11-7 and fair lending obligations. A generative AI tool used with member data triggers GLBA. This mapping becomes the regulatory risk dimension of your AI risk assessment.

2. Review vendor contracts for AI-related provisions. Identify whether contracts address model validation documentation, data handling and retention by the vendor, notification obligations if the AI model changes materially, and the institution's right to audit or request model transparency documentation.

3. Develop a brief regulatory landscape briefing for the board. Leadership does not need to understand the technical details of SR 11-7 or the FFIEC handbook. They need to understand that regulatory expectations exist, that the institution has exposure, and that a governance program is being developed to address it.

4. Document your current AI governance posture against examiner expectations. Even if the documentation reveals significant gaps, a candid gap analysis is more defensible than an absence of self-assessment. Examiners respond more favorably to institutions that have identified their gaps and have a remediation plan than to institutions that appear unaware of the issue.

5. Establish a process for monitoring regulatory developments. NCUA letters to credit unions, FFIEC handbook updates, and interagency guidance releases should be reviewed for AI-related content regularly. Assign this monitoring responsibility to a named individual.

Important Points

- There is no single AI regulation for credit unions; AI governance obligations are distributed across SR 11-7, the FFIEC IT Handbook, GLBA, consumer protection law, and emerging interagency guidance.
- Existing regulatory frameworks apply to AI activities, whether they mention AI explicitly. The absence of an AI-specific rule does not mean the absence of a regulatory obligation.
- NCUA examiners are actively incorporating AI governance into technology and risk examinations. Institutions without a documented program are creating examination exposure.
- Vendor AI does not transfer regulatory responsibility to the vendor. The institution remains accountable for AI-driven decisions that affect members, including decisions made by third-party models.
- Institutions that build their AI governance programs against established frameworks, particularly SR 11-7 and the NIST AI RMF, are building on a foundation that regulators have explicitly endorsed and will recognize in examinations.

Questions for Leadership

1. Have we reviewed our AI activities against SR 11-7 model risk management expectations, including vendor-side validation documentation?

2. Do our vendor contracts for AI-enabled platforms include provisions for model transparency, data handling, and material change notification?
3. Have we assessed whether any AI systems in our environment create fair lending or consumer protection exposure?
4. Does the board understand the regulatory landscape for AI, and has that understanding been documented in board meeting minutes?
5. Do we have a process in place to monitor regulatory developments in AI governance and update our program in response?

Further Reading

- SR 11-7: Supervisory Guidance on Model Risk Management—Federal Reserve Board/OCC (2011)
- FFIEC IT Examination Handbook, Third-Party Relationships Booklet—Federal Financial Institutions Examination Council
- GLBA Safeguards Rule, 16 CFR Part 314 (2021 Amendments)—Federal Trade Commission
- Interagency Request for Information on AI in Financial Services—OCC, Fed, FDIC, NCUA, CFPB (2023)
- NIST AI Risk Management Framework (AI RMF 1.0), GOVERN and MAP Functions—NIST

PART II

Preparing for Responsible AI Adoption

Chapters 4–6 address preparation: how to evaluate AI before deployment, how to conduct a structured risk assessment, and how to apply the AI Vendor Risk Evaluation Model to third-party relationships.

CHAPTER 4

Evaluating AI Before Deployment

Opening Scenario

The request came through the normal IT intake process, flagged as a routine software evaluation. The mortgage lending team wanted to pilot a new loan origination platform from a vendor they had been speaking with for several months. The vendor had shown the product twice; the lending VP was enthusiastic, and the projected efficiency gains were significant. The ask from IT was straightforward: review the platform, confirm security requirements, and schedule a proof of concept.

The Information Security Program Manager (ISPM) pulled up the vendor's product sheet and immediately noticed something the lending team had not flagged: the platform included an AI-powered underwriting decision support module. It was described in marketing language as a "smart recommendation engine" that analyzed application data against historical loan performance patterns to surface risk indicators and suggest disposition options for loan officers.

This was not a writing assistant. This was a system that would analyze member financial data, compare it against model-trained patterns, and produce recommendations that would directly inform credit decisions affecting real members. The risk profile of this tool was categorically different from the productivity software that the intake form had implied.

B. A. Salas, *AI Risk Management for Financial Institutions*,
https://doi.org/10.1007/979-8-8688-3353-3_4

The ISPM paused the evaluation and sent the lending VP a note. He needed two things before the pilot could proceed: the vendor's model documentation, including training data sources, validation methodology, and fair lending testing results; and a completed AI risk assessment using the institution's classification framework.

The lending VP pushed back gently. Other credit unions were already using the platform. The vendor had strong references. The pilot would only take sixty days.

The ISPM understood the pressure. He also understood that "other credit unions are using it" was not a risk assessment. It was a procurement argument. It was, in his experience, the governance equivalent of "everyone else was speeding too." The fact that other institutions had deployed a system without fully evaluating it was not a reason to do the same; it was, if anything, a reason to be more deliberate. He held the line. The evaluation proceeded with the documentation requests in place.

What came back from the vendor was illuminating. The model had not been tested for disparate impact against the credit union's specific member demographics. The training data was from a national dataset that skewed toward urban lending patterns. And the vendor's terms of service included a clause that allowed the model to be retrained using customer data unless the institution opted out, a clause buried seventeen pages into the contract.

The pilot was eventually approved, with conditions. But only because someone had asked the right questions before the system went live.

The Risk Problem

The moment when an AI system is easiest to govern is before it is deployed. Once a system is live, once workflows have been built around it, staff have been trained on it, and its outputs have affected members, the governance conversation becomes reactive. Pre-deployment evaluation is the point in the lifecycle where the institution has the most leverage: it can ask questions, demand documentation, negotiate contract terms, and make a deliberate go or no-go decision before any risk is accepted.

Most institutions under-invest in pre-deployment evaluation for AI for two reasons. First, AI capabilities often arrive embedded in systems that are being evaluated for non-AI reasons: a new lending platform, an updated fraud detection module, or a refreshed member service tool. The AI component is not the headline feature, and it may not be prominently disclosed. Second, the urgency of business units to deploy efficiency-gaining technology creates pressure to move quickly through evaluation processes that feel like obstacles rather than safeguards.

The risk of inadequate pre-deployment evaluation is not hypothetical. It is the accumulation of unknown risks: unknown model behavior, unknown data handling practices, unknown fair lending exposure, and unknown contractual obligations. Each unknown is a potential examination finding, a potential member harm, or a potential incident waiting for the conditions that will surface it. A note on sequencing: pre-deployment evaluation governs AI systems before they enter the environment. For most credit unions beginning their governance work, the majority of AI systems they will first encounter are already in use. The inventory and discovery process that surfaces those systems is covered in Chapter 7. The framework in this chapter applies to every new AI system from the point the governance program is established forward—and retroactively to unapproved systems identified through inventory, which should receive a structured evaluation as part of their governance triage.

Why It Matters to Credit Unions

Credit unions typically operate with lean procurement and technology evaluation teams. The ISPM, the CRO, or the Compliance Officer who handles AI evaluation is usually the same person responsible for a dozen other program areas. That resource reality does not eliminate the obligation to evaluate AI before deployment; it makes a structured and efficient evaluation framework essential.

A well-designed pre-deployment evaluation process does not require weeks of analysis for every AI tool. It requires a classification step that determines how much evaluation is proportionate to the risk level of the system. A Level 1 informational AI tool, a writing assistant used internally with no member data, requires a different level of scrutiny than a Level 3 decision support system recommending loan dispositions. The evaluation framework scales with the risk.

For credit unions, pre-deployment evaluation also serves as a relationship function with business units. A consistent, documented process that business units can expect and prepare for causes far less friction than ad hoc security reviews that arrive as surprises late in a procurement process. When the ISPM is seen as a structured partner in AI adoption rather than a last-minute obstacle, the institution's ability to govern AI improves across the board.

Governance and Risk Considerations

Effective pre-deployment evaluation of AI requires two foundational capabilities: a classification model that calibrates the evaluation effort to the risk level of the system, and a structured evaluation checklist that ensures consistent coverage of key risk domains. The AI Risk Classification Model provides the first capability.

The AI Risk Classification Model

The AI Risk Classification Model organizes AI systems into four levels based on their function, their proximity to consequential decisions, and their use of member data. The level assigned to a system determines the depth and formality of the evaluation required before deployment is approved.

RISK LEVEL	EXAMPLES	RISK RATING
Level 1 Informational AI	Writing assistants, document summarization, meeting transcription	Low
Level 2 Operational AI	Fraud analysis support, ticket triage, customer service assistance	Moderate
Level 3 Decision Support AI	Loan underwriting models, fraud detection scoring, and financial forecasting	High
Level 4 Autonomous AI	Automated underwriting, automated account actions, compliance decisions	Critical

Figure 4-1. *The AI Risk Classification Model—four levels calibrating evaluation depth and oversight requirements*

Level 1: Informational AI

Level 1 systems support productivity and information tasks. They do not make decisions about members, and staff typically use them internally. The primary risk at this level is data exposure: does the tool have access to member data, and if so, how is that data handled? A writing assistant used to draft internal memos carries minimal risk. The same tool used to draft member communications with personal financial details pasted into the prompt requires a different evaluation.

Pre-deployment evaluation for Level 1 systems should confirm whether the tool accesses or keeps member data, whether staff use is bounded by a clear acceptable use policy, whether the vendor's data handling terms are compatible with GLBA obligations, and whether the tool has been communicated to IT, so it is not operating as shadow AI.

Level 2: Operational AI

Level 2 systems support operational workflows. They may interact with member data, surface recommendations to staff, or automate routine classification and routing tasks. The risk at this level includes data exposure, operational dependency, and the potential for AI-driven triage decisions to systematically route member interactions in ways that create service equity concerns.

Pre-deployment evaluation for Level 2 systems should include everything in Level 1, plus: a review of how the system's outputs are used by staff, whether staff can override or correct AI recommendations, what data the system ingests and retains, and whether the vendor has documented the model's behavior and limitations.

Level 3: Decision Support AI

Level 3 systems directly inform consequential decisions affecting members: lending, fraud, and financial forecasting. These systems carry the highest routine governance burden because their outputs are closest to the outcomes that matter most to members and to regulators. Fair lending exposure, model opacity, and the risk that model recommendations displace rather than support human judgment are the primary concerns at this level.

Pre-deployment evaluation for Level 3 systems requires the full evaluation framework: model documentation and validation evidence from the vendor, fair lending and disparate impact testing results, data handling and retention terms, the institution's right to challenge or audit model outputs, staff training requirements, ongoing monitoring commitments, and formal risk assessment documentation before the system is approved for use.

Level 4: Autonomous AI

Level 4 systems act without a human review of individual decisions. Automated underwriting that renders final decisions, automated account actions triggered by AI behavioral scoring, and automated compliance flags that result in account restrictions without human review all operate at this level. The risk is highest because the human check that catches model errors before they affect members has been removed from the loop.

Level 4 deployment requires the most rigorous pre-deployment process and the most explicit board or executive approval. It also requires ongoing monitoring that is more frequent and more sensitive than lower-level systems, and a clearly defined process for identifying and remediating systematic model errors before they accumulate into a pattern of member harm.

Classification in Practice Not every AI system arrives with a clear level label. When classifying a new system, ask two questions:

1. Does this system touch member data or inform decisions about members?
2. Does a human review and keep authority over the final decision, or does the system act autonomously?

If the answer to question 1 is no, the system is likely Level 1.

If the answer to question 2 is that a human retains authority, the system is Level 2 or 3.

If the system acts without prior human review, it is Level 4.

When in doubt, classify higher and scale back after further evaluation, not the reverse.

The Pre-Deployment Evaluation Checklist

Regardless of classification level, a structured pre-deployment evaluation should address five domains: purpose and function, data handling, model transparency, vendor accountability, and operational readiness. The depth of evaluation in each domain scales with the classification level.

- **Purpose and function**: What does the system do? What decisions does it inform or make? Who uses it and in what workflows? Does the stated purpose match the vendor's actual product capabilities?
- **Data handling**: What member or institutional data does the system ingest? Where is that data processed and stored? Does the vendor retain data for model training? Are data handling terms contractually documented and compatible with GLBA?
- **Model transparency**: Can the vendor explain how the model reaches its outputs? Has the model been validated? Has it been tested for bias or disparate impact? Are the model's limitations documented?
- **Vendor accountability**: What are the vendor's obligations if the model behaves unexpectedly? Does the contract include notification requirements for material model changes? Does the institution have audit rights?
- **Operational readiness**: Are staff trained to use the system appropriately, including understanding its limitations? Is there a process for staff to flag and escalate AI outputs that appear incorrect? Is ongoing monitoring defined?

Implementation Steps

1. Integrate AI classification into your existing technology intake process. Add a simple question to your IT intake or vendor evaluation form: Does this system use AI or machine learning in any component? A yes answer triggers the AI evaluation track.
2. Build a one-page AI classification reference card for use by business units and IT staff. The card should describe the four levels, give two or three examples of each, and specify what evaluation is required at each level. Make the process visible and accessible before someone needs it.
3. Develop a tiered evaluation checklist with the five domains above. Create a lightweight version for Level 1 systems that can be completed in under an hour, and a more comprehensive version for Level 3 and Level 4 systems that includes formal vendor documentation requests.
4. Establish an approval authority matrix for AI deployment. The ISPM might approve Level 1 AI systems independently. Level 2 by the ISPM and CRO jointly. Level 3 by the Risk Committee. Level 4 by an executive leadership with board notification. The matrix makes accountability explicit before an evaluation begins.

5. Document every pre-deployment evaluation, regardless of the outcome. The documentation is both your institutional memory and your examination evidence. An examiner who sees a consistent record of AI evaluations, even simple ones for Level 1 systems, sees an institution that takes governance seriously.

Important Points

- Pre-deployment is the highest leverage point in the AI governance lifecycle. The institution has the most control before a system is live and workflows are built around it.
- The AI Risk Classification Model assigns systems to one of four levels: Informational, Operational, Decision Support, or Autonomous, based on their function and proximity to consequential member decisions.
- Evaluation depth scales with the classification level. Level 1 requires a lightweight data handling check. Level 4 requires formal documentation, fair lending testing evidence, and executive approval.
- AI capabilities frequently arrive embedded in systems evaluated for non-AI reasons. The intake process must ask the AI questions explicitly rather than waiting for it to be disclosed.
- When classification is uncertain, default to the higher level. Scaling back after further evaluation is safer than under-evaluating a system that turns out to carry more risk than initially apparent.

Questions for Leadership

1. Does our technology intake process currently ask whether a system includes AI or machine learning capabilities, and does a yes answer trigger a defined evaluation track?
2. Have we classified all currently deployed AI systems using a risk-level framework, and does that classification inform how we govern and monitor them?
3. For any Level 3 or Level 4 systems currently in use, do we have vendor documentation of model validation and fair lending testing on file?
4. Is there a defined approval authority for AI deployment decisions, and does that authority scale appropriately with the risk level of the system?
5. Are business unit leaders aware of the AI evaluation process and their role in it before they begin vendor conversations?

Further Reading

- SR 11-7: Supervisory Guidance on Model Risk Management, Section on Model Validation—Federal Reserve Board/OCC.
- NIST AI RMF, MAP Function: Categorize and Analyze AI Risks—National Institute of Standards and Technology.

- CFPB Guidance on Adverse Action Notices and Algorithmic Decision-Making—Consumer Financial Protection Bureau.
- FFIEC IT Examination Handbook, Development and Acquisition Booklet—Federal Financial Institutions Examination Council.
- NCUA Letter 21-CU-08: Third-Party Relationships—National Credit Union Administration.

CHAPTER 5

AI Risk Assessment Foundations

Opening Scenario

The Risk Committee meeting had been on the calendar for three weeks. The Information Security Program Manager (ISPM) had requested thirty minutes to present the institution's first formal AI risk assessment, a structured evaluation of the four AI systems the inventory process had identified. He had spent two weeks building the assessment, drawing on vendor documentation, staff interviews, and a review of applicable regulatory guidance.

He opened with the AI Governance Pyramid and reminded the committee where risk assessment sat in the overall structure: Layer 3, above the operational controls they had been building and below the governance program they were working toward. Then he walked through the four systems one at a time.

The first was the fraud detection module embedded in the core platform, a Level 3 system under the classification model. The vendor had provided partial model documentation but had declined to share training data provenance, citing proprietary concerns. Fair lending testing results existed, but covered a national dataset that did not reflect the

B. A. Salas, *AI Risk Management for Financial Institutions*,
https://doi.org/10.1007/979-8-8688-3353-3_5

credit union's membership demographics. The ISPM rated this system as having high residual risk pending additional vendor documentation and a demographic-specific disparate impact review.

The second was the generative AI tool that three members of the marketing team had been using informally. It was a Level 1 system in terms of function, but the team had been pasting member demographic language into prompts to personalize campaign copy. That data handling behavior elevated the actual risk profile above what the tool's classification alone suggested. The ISPM rated this as a moderate risk and recommended an immediate acceptable use policy and staff retraining before continued use.

The third was the AI-powered ticket triage system in member services; a Level 2 system operating largely as designed, with reasonable vendor documentation and no member data kept beyond the session. Low residual risk, with a recommendation for quarterly monitoring.

The fourth was a new automated underwriting pilot that the lending team had proposed for the coming quarter. They had not yet deployed the system. The ISPM had classified it as Level 4 and recommended a full evaluation process, including board notification, before any pilot approval was granted.

Upon completion, the Risk Committee chair posed the question ISPM desired: "What actions must this committee undertake because of this assessment?" It was the right question. That was the point of the exercise.

The Risk Problem

Risk assessment is the mechanism by which an institution translates AI inventory into its risk posture. Without it, knowing that AI systems exist in the environment produces no governance outcome. This inventory responds to the query, "What is present?" The risk assessment answers the questions that matter to leadership and examiners: how risky is it, what are we doing about it, and is the residual risk acceptable?

The risk problem at this layer of the governance pyramid is twofold. First, many institutions conflate AI evaluation, the pre-deployment review covered in Chapter 4, with ongoing risk assessment. Evaluation is a gate. Risk assessment is a continuous process. A system that passed its pre-deployment evaluation with acceptable risk may evolve as the vendor keeps the model, as the institution's use of the system expands, or as the regulatory environment around it changes. Risk assessment must be periodic, not a onetime event.

Second, AI risk assessment requires a different methodology than conventional IT risk assessment. The risks are not primarily about system availability or access controls, though those matter too. The primary risks in AI systems involve model behavior: whether the system produces accurate, fair, and explainable outputs; whether those outputs are being used appropriately by staff; and whether the institution can detect and respond when something goes wrong. Those risks require assessment criteria that most standard IT risk frameworks do not include by default.

Why It Matters to Credit Unions

For credit unions, the AI risk assessment serves three simultaneous purposes. It is a governance tool; it produces the risk information leadership needs to make informed decisions. It is a compliance tool; it creates the documentation that examiners ask for when they assess whether the institution's AI program is defensible. And it is an operational tool; it surfaces the specific remediation actions needed to bring risk to acceptable levels.

A well-executed AI risk assessment also builds institutional credibility for the security and risk program. When an ISPM presents a structured, evidence-based risk picture to the Risk Committee or the board, the credibility of the program increases. Leadership that understands the risk is better positioned to resource the program, support necessary vendor negotiations, and engage with examiner questions from a position of informed awareness rather than reactive uncertainty.

A credit union with three AI systems does not need the same assessment infrastructure as an institution with thirty. But every system needs a documented assessment. The depth scales with the system; the discipline does not.

Governance and Risk Considerations

A sound AI risk assessment methodology addresses four dimensions for each system in scope: inherent risk, control effectiveness, residual risk, and risk disposition. These dimensions are not unique to AI; they apply to enterprise risk assessment broadly, but the criteria used to evaluate each dimension must be calibrated to the specific characteristics of AI systems.

Dimension 1: Inherent Risk

Inherent risk is the risk a system carries before any controls are applied. For AI systems, inherent risk is primarily a function of four factors: the classification level of the system (Level 1 through Level 4, as established in Chapter 4), the sensitivity of the data the system processes, the degree to which the system's outputs inform or make consequential decisions, and the opacity of the underlying model.

A Level 3 system that processes member financial data to produce loan recommendations starts with high inherent risk. A Level 1 tool used internally with no member data starts with low inherent risk. The classification level provides the baseline; the data sensitivity and decision impact dimensions adjust it. A system can be functionally Level 2 but carry Level 3 inherent risk if it processes unusually sensitive data or if its outputs are being used in ways that approach autonomous decision-making in practice.

Dimension 2: Control Effectiveness

Control effectiveness measures how well the institution's existing controls address the inherent risk of the system. For AI systems, relevant controls include: vendor contract provisions that establish data handling obligations and model transparency requirements; staff-acceptable use policies that govern how AI outputs are used; human oversight mechanisms that ensure staff can review, challenge, and override AI recommendations; monitoring processes that track system behavior over time; and incident response capabilities that apply when AI-related anomalies are detected.

Control effectiveness is not binary. A control that exists on paper but has not been operationalized, tested, or communicated to staff provides less actual risk reduction than a control that is actively enforced and periodically verified. The assessment should evaluate whether controls are designed appropriately and whether they are functioning as intended in practice.

Dimension 3: Residual Risk

Residual risk is the risk that remains after controls have been applied. It is the number that matters to leadership: how much risk are we actually carrying for this system today? Residual risk is expressed as the combination of inherent risk and control effectiveness; high inherent risk with firm controls may produce moderate residual risk; low inherent risk with weak controls may produce the same.

For AI systems, residual risk frequently includes a component that cannot be fully mitigated: model opacity. If the institution cannot obtain sufficient documentation from a vendor to understand how a model makes decisions, there is a floor below which residual risk cannot be reduced, regardless of what controls are in place. That floor should be made explicit in the assessment and presented to leadership as an acceptable or unacceptable condition.

Dimension 4: Risk Disposition

Risk disposition is the institution's decision about what to do with the residual risk identified. The standard enterprise risk options apply: accept the risk as within appetite, mitigate through additional controls, transfer through contractual or insurance mechanisms, or avoid by discontinuing use of the system. For AI systems, a fifth option is often appropriate: accept conditionally, pending specific remediation actions within a defined time frame.

Conditional acceptance is the most common risk disposition for AI systems in active use. The institution is not willing to discontinue a system that is delivering operational value, but the current residual risk is above its appetite. The assessment documents the gap, defines the remediation actions required to close it, assigns ownership, and sets a deadline. The Risk Committee reviews progress at the next assessment cycle.

AI Risk Assessment: Key Criteria by Dimension Inherent Risk: Classification level • Data sensitivity • Decision impact • Model opacity

Control Effectiveness: Vendor contract terms • Acceptable use policy • Human oversight mechanisms • Monitoring processes • Incident response coverage

Residual Risk: Inherent risk adjusted for control effectiveness • Irreducible opacity floor

---

Risk Disposition: Accept • Mitigate • Transfer • Avoid • Accept conditionally with a defined remediation timeline and ownership

Assessment Frequency and Triggers

AI risk assessments should be conducted on a defined periodic schedule and triggered by specific events. Periodic assessment frequency should correspond to classification level: Level 1 systems annually, Level 2 systems semi-annually, Level 3 and Level 4 systems quarterly or at each significant vendor update cycle.

Event-based triggers that should initiate an out-of-cycle assessment include: notification from a vendor that the model has been materially updated or retrained; an AI-related incident or near-miss; a material change in how the institution uses the system; a change in the regulatory landscape that affects the system's risk profile; and the results of staff feedback or monitoring that suggest the system is behaving differently than documented.

The assessment schedule and trigger criteria should be documented in the institution's AI governance policy so that they are not dependent on an individual judgment about when a reassessment is warranted. When the criteria are explicit, the question of whether to reassess becomes administrative rather than discretionary.

Documentation Standards

The output of an AI risk assessment is a documented record that supports both internal governance decisions and external examination review. At a minimum, each assessment record should include: the system name, vendor, and classification level; the assessment date and the next scheduled assessment date; the inherent risk rating with supporting rationale; the controls evaluated and their effectiveness rating; the residual risk rating with supporting rationale; the risk disposition decision with ownership and timeline if remediation is required; and the name of the individual who conducted the assessment and the governance body that reviewed it.

Documentation does not need to be lengthy to be defensible. A well-structured one- or two-page assessment record for a Level 1 system is more valuable than a twenty-page report that was never reviewed by leadership. The standard is clarity, completeness, and evidence of governance engagement, not volume.

Implementation Steps

1. Develop an AI risk assessment template calibrated to your classification levels. Create a lightweight template for Level 1 and Level 2 systems and a more detailed template for Level 3 and Level 4 systems. Both should address all four assessment dimensions. Templates reduce the time required per assessment and ensure consistent coverage across systems.
2. Conduct an initial risk assessment for every AI system in your current inventory. Prioritize by classification level; assess Level 3 and Level 4 systems first. Document inherent risk, control effectiveness, residual risk, and risk disposition for each. Treat the first round as a baseline from which subsequent assessments will measure change.
3. Establish assessment ownership. The ISPM typically owns the assessment process and produces the initial assessment. The Risk Committee reviews and formally accepts or escalates the risk disposition decisions. For Level 4 systems, executive leadership should be in the review chain. Document the ownership and review chain in your AI governance policy.

4. Build assessment frequency into your governance calendar. Add AI risk assessment reviews to the Risk Committee agenda on the schedule that corresponds to your system classification levels. Treat them as standing agenda items rather than ad hoc presentations. Consistency signals program maturity to examiners.

5. Create a remediation tracking process. Documented tracking of remediation progress must follow risk assessments that identify gaps requiring remediation. A simple log that records the gap, the required action, the owner, the due date, and the current status is sufficient. Review open remediation items at each Risk Committee meeting.

Important Points

- Risk assessment translates AI inventory into risk posture: it answers not just what is here but how risky it is, what is being done about it, and whether the residual risk is acceptable.
- AI risk assessment is a continuous process, not a onetime gate. Systems evolve through vendor retraining and expanded use. Assessment must be periodic and event-triggered.
- The four assessment dimensions—inherent risk, control effectiveness, residual risk, and risk disposition—apply to every system in the inventory, with evaluation depth scaling to classification level.

- Model opacity creates a residual risk floor that cannot be fully mitigated through controls. That floor must be made explicit in the assessment and accepted or challenged by leadership as a governance decision.
- Documentation standards matter more than documentation volume. A clear, complete, reviewed assessment record for every system is the defensible examination outcome, not a lengthy report that was never presented to a governance body.

Questions for Leadership

1. Have we completed a formal risk assessment for every AI system currently in our inventory, including systems that arrived through vendor updates rather than deliberate deployment decisions?
2. Does our risk assessment methodology address model behavior risks, accuracy, fairness, and explainability, or does it apply only standard IT risk criteria?
3. For any AI system with high or critical residual risk, has the Risk Committee reviewed and formally accepted or escalated the risk disposition decision?
4. Do we have a defined assessment schedule that corresponds to system classification levels, and is that schedule reflected in the Risk Committee's standing agenda?

5. Are open remediation items from prior AI risk assessments being tracked, and is progress against those items reviewed at each Risk Committee meeting?

Further Reading

- NIST AI RMF, MEASURE Function: Analyze and Assess AI Risks—National Institute of Standards and Technology.
- SR 11-7: Supervisory Guidance on Model Risk Management, Ongoing Monitoring Section—Federal Reserve Board/OCC.
- FFIEC IT Examination Handbook, Management Booklet, Risk Assessment Section—Federal Financial Institutions Examination Council.
- ISO/IEC 23894:2023—AI Risk Management Guidance.
- NCUA Examiner's Guide, Information Systems and Technology National Credit Union Administration.

CHAPTER 6

AI Vendor Due Diligence

Opening Scenario

The vendor management review had been on the schedule for two months. The credit union's contract with its core platform provider was up for renewal, and the Information Security Program Manager (ISPM) had been tasked with completing the periodic third-party risk assessment before the renewal was signed. He had done this before: the standard questionnaire, the SOC 2 report review, the business continuity documentation. It was familiar territory.

What was less familiar was the addendum the vendor had submitted alongside the renewal agreement. Three new AI-powered modules were being bundled into the platform at no additional cost: an AI-assisted member onboarding verification tool, an anomaly detection module for fraud monitoring, and a "smart routing" feature that would use behavioral analysis to direct member service inquiries to the appropriate support channel.

The standard vendor questionnaire had no questions about any of these capabilities. The SOC 2 report predated their introduction. And the business continuity documentation described the platform as if it had existed eighteen months ago. The ISPM was looking at three new

B. A. Salas, *AI Risk Management for Financial Institutions*,
https://doi.org/10.1007/979-8-8688-3353-3_6

AI systems, two of them touching member data and one informing fraud decisions, which his existing due diligence framework was not equipped to evaluate.

He pulled out the AI Vendor Risk Evaluation Model he had been developing and worked through each system against its four risk categories. The member onboarding tool raised data exposure concerns immediately: the vendor's documentation showed that verification data, including identity document images, was processed by a third-party AI sub-processor that the primary vendor had not disclosed in prior assessments. The anomaly detection module had no published validation method and no disparate impact testing results on file. The smart routing feature was the least concerning of the three; it did not touch sensitive data, and its outputs were purely operational, but it still warranted documentation and inclusion in the AI inventory.

The ISPM went back to the vendor with eleven specific questions. The renewal was delayed by six weeks. Two of the questions produced contractual addenda that the institution's legal counsel considered significant protections. One produced a disclosure about sub-processor data handling that triggered a conversation with compliance about GLBA notification obligations.

Six weeks of delay. Eleven questions. Two contract improvements. One compliance flag. That was the value of AI-specific vendor due diligence applied to a routine contract renewal.

The Risk Problem

Vendor due diligence programs at most credit unions were designed for a world where the primary risks in third-party relationships were operational continuity, data security, and contractual performance. Those risks remain relevant. AI-enabled vendors, however, introduce a risk category that standard due diligence frameworks fail to surface: the risk that the vendor's AI systems behave in ways the institution cannot predict, explain to members, or defend to examiners.

The fundamental challenge is asymmetrical. The vendor built the model, controlled the training data, determined when to retrain the model, and decided how much documentation to share with customers. The institution uses the model's outputs to make decisions, or allows the model to decide autonomously, without meaningful visibility into how those outputs are produced. In a non-AI vendor relationship, the institution at least knows how the software works in principle. With an AI model, the institution often cannot explain the relationship between the inputs and the outputs even in principle.

That asymmetry is a governance problem, a regulatory problem, and a member trust problem simultaneously. Due diligence is the institution's primary mechanism for closing the information gap before the contract is signed and the system is deployed. After establishing the relationship, the institution has less leverage to demand transparency.

Why It Matters to Credit Unions

Credit unions rely heavily on vendor technology. The core platform, the lending system, the fraud detection infrastructure, and the member communication tools; most of these are vendor-provided, and most are now AI-enabled in at least some capacity. The vendor portfolio is not a peripheral concern for AI governance. It is the primary surface through which AI risk enters the institution.

NCUA's guidance on third-party relationships establishes that the institution is responsible for vendor actions affecting members or institutional safety and soundness—a principle that applies with full force to AI-enabled vendors. The institution's vendor oversight obligations extend fully into the AI capabilities those vendors deploy, and the AI Vendor Risk Evaluation Model is the structured mechanism for meeting that obligation.

For small security teams, the practical implication is that AI vendor due diligence must be integrated into the existing vendor management program rather than operated as a separate process. The institution cannot afford to run parallel oversight systems. The AI-specific questions and evaluation criteria must be layered into the standard vendor review workflow so that they are applied consistently without requiring additional overhead for each review cycle.

Governance and Risk Considerations

The AI Vendor Risk Evaluation Model provides the framework for conducting AI-specific due diligence. It organizes vendor AI risk into four categories, each of which requires specific inquiry during the due diligence process and ongoing monitoring during the vendor relationship.

The AI Vendor Risk Evaluation Model

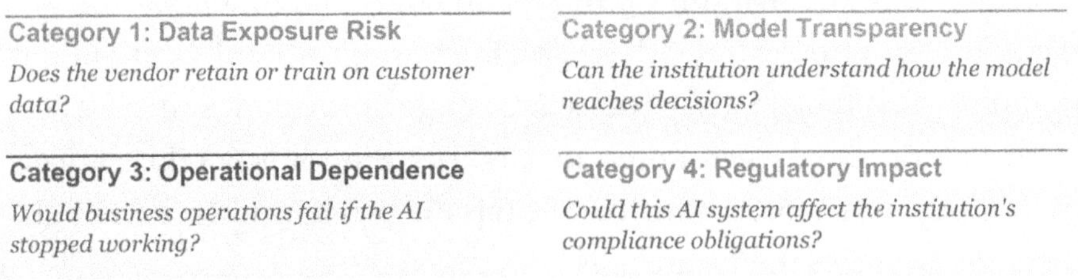

Figure 6-1. *The AI Vendor Risk Evaluation Model—four categories for AI-specific due diligence*

Category 1: Data Exposure Risk

Data exposure risk addresses whether the vendor's AI capabilities create unauthorized or unintended access to, retention of, or use of member data. This is the most immediately tangible risk category for most credit unions, and it is the one most directly implicated by the GLBA Safeguards Rule obligations.

Key due diligence questions for this category include: Does the vendor's AI model process member data, and if so, where is that processing performed? Does the vendor keep member data used in AI processing, for how long, and under what data governance controls? Does the vendor use member data, or outputs derived from member data, to train or improve its AI models? Are there sub-processors involved in AI data handling that are not disclosed in the primary vendor agreement? What contractual protections govern the vendor's data handling obligations, and are those protections specific to AI processing?

The sub-processor question deserves particular attention. AI model inference and training frequently involve cloud infrastructure providers, specialized AI platform vendors, or third-party model providers that sit behind the primary vendor relationship. The institution's GLBA obligations flow through to those sub-processors, but the contractual chain that establishes that obligation is only as strong as the primary vendor agreement that creates it.

Category 2: Model Transparency

Model transparency addresses whether the institution can develop a sufficient understanding of how the vendor's AI model functions to exercise meaningful oversight. Full transparency, access to training data, model architecture, and inference logic, is rarely available from commercial vendors and is not the standard the institution should demand. The standard is functional transparency: enough understanding of what the model does, what data it uses, what its documented limitations are, and how it has been validated to allow the institution to use it responsibly and challenge its outputs when warranted.

Key due diligence questions include: Has the vendor conducted validation of the model, and is validation documentation available? What are the model's documented limitations and known failure modes? Has the model been tested for bias, disparate impact, or demographic performance differences, and are those results available? How does the vendor explain model decisions to affected individuals when required? What is the vendor's process for notifying customers when the model is materially updated or retrained? Does the institution have any contractual right to audit model performance or request updated validation documentation?

A vendor that cannot answer these questions, or that answers them only with marketing language rather than technical documentation, is presenting a model transparency risk that the institution must weigh against the operational value of the system. Sometimes, the answer is to proceed with appropriate contractual protection and monitoring. In others, the opacity suffices to make the system unsuitable for the use case, regardless of its commercial appeal.

Category 3: Operational Dependence

Operational dependence addresses the risk that the institution's business processes become so reliant on a vendor's AI capabilities that a disruption to those capabilities creates a material operational impact. This risk is distinct from general business continuity risk because AI systems can degrade gradually rather than fail completely; a model that begins producing lower-quality outputs after a retraining event may not trigger the same alerts as a system outage, but its impact on operations can be equally significant.

Key due diligence questions include: What manual processes exist if the AI system becomes unavailable? How quickly could the institution revert to non-AI workflows, and what would the operational impact of that reversion be? Does the vendor's SLA cover AI-specific performance metrics, or only system availability? What is the vendor's process for communicating AI system degradation that does not rise to the level of an outage? Is the institution's dependency on this AI system reflected in its business continuity and disaster recovery planning?

Operational dependence risk compounds over time. A system that is initially used as a decision support tool can evolve into an effectively autonomous system as staff become accustomed to accepting its recommendations without challenge. Monitoring this drift and maintaining staff capability to operate independently of AI tools is both a governance obligation and a business continuity requirement.

Category 4: Regulatory Impact

Regulatory impact addresses whether the vendor's AI capabilities create or change the institution's compliance obligations. This category is distinct from the others because the risk is not primarily operational; it is about whether using the system changes what the institution is required to do from a regulatory standpoint.

Key due diligence questions include: Does the system's use of AI in lending or account decisions trigger adverse action notice requirements under ECOA or FCRA? Does the system's handling of member data create obligations under state privacy laws that supplement GLBA? Does the vendor's AI capability make up a model under SR 11-7, and if so, what validation documentation does the institution need to maintain on file? Has the vendor represented to regulators that their product supports compliance with specific requirements, and are those representations consistent with how the institution intends to use the system?

Regulatory impact assessment requires coordination between the ISPM, the compliance officer, and, in complex cases, legal counsel. The ISPM is best positioned to identify the technical capabilities that create regulatory exposure; the compliance officer is best positioned to assess what those capabilities require under applicable law. AI vendor due diligence is one of the clearest examples in the security program of a function that cannot be performed effectively in isolation. The regulatory impact dimension also intersects with the responsible AI framework addressed in Chapter 17: a vendor whose AI produces discriminatory outcomes creates both a regulatory violation and a values failure for which the institution bears accountability, regardless of where the model was built.

Integrating AI Due Diligence into Existing Vendor Management

The AI Vendor Risk Evaluation Model does not replace existing vendor management processes. It extends to them. The practical integration points are:

- New vendor evaluations: Add AI capability discovery questions to the initial questionnaire.
- Contract negotiation: Use the four risk categories to drive AI-specific contract provisions.
- Periodic reviews: Add AI risk category reassessment to the annual or biennial vendor review.
- Contract renewals: Treat renewed contracts as new evaluations when AI capabilities have been added or materially changed since the prior review.

AI-Specific Contract Provisions

Due diligence produces information. Contract negotiation translates that information into enforceable protections. For AI-enabled vendors, the institution should pursue specific contractual provisions that address the four risk categories above. Some vendors may not meet every stipulation. Large platform vendors with standard terms have limited flexibility, but the attempt to get these provisions, and the vendor's response to that attempt, is itself meaningful due diligence information.

Provisions worth pursuing include: explicit data handling obligations covering AI processing and sub-processors; prohibition on using member data for model training without written consent; material change notification requirements triggered by model retraining or significant capability changes; documentation delivery obligations for validation results and bias testing; audit rights covering AI-specific performance metrics; liability provisions that address AI-related member harm; and a right to terminate for cause if the vendor's AI system produces documented discriminatory outcomes that the vendor cannot remediate.

Implementation Steps

1. Audit your current vendor portfolio for AI capabilities. For every active vendor relationship, determine whether the vendor's platform includes any AI or machine learning functionality. This does not require deep technical investigation; a review of the product documentation and a direct inquiry to your vendor account manager for each relationship suffices to establish the baseline.

2. Add the four AI risk categories to your standard vendor questionnaire. Create four to six questions for each category: data exposure, model transparency, operational dependence, and regulatory impact, and add them as a conditional section that activates when a vendor confirms AI capabilities are present.

3. Prioritize AI due diligence for upcoming renewals and new procurements. You cannot retroactively renegotiate every existing contract simultaneously. Focus the initial AI due diligence effort on contracts coming up for renewal and new vendor evaluations, where the institution has the most leverage.

4. Develop a standard set of AI contract provisions and share them with legal counsel. Legal review of AI contract language is most efficient when counsel has a baseline set of provisions to work from rather than evaluating AI risk from first principles in each negotiation. Build the standard provisions once; refine them as vendor negotiations produce feedback.

5. Document due diligence outcomes in your vendor risk register. Each vendor with AI capabilities should have a record that captures the four risk category assessments, the contract provisions obtained, the provisions that were declined, and any residual risk accepted. Some examples of this would be agent permissions and the risk associated with that access, or any risk that was deemed acceptable when accessing member data via automation. That being said, this documentation is both your institutional memory and your examination evidence for vendor oversight.

Important Points

- The vendor portfolio is the primary surface through which AI risk enters most credit unions. Vendor due diligence is the institution's most important AI risk control at the point of relationship establishment.
- The AI Vendor Risk Evaluation Model organizes vendor AI risk into four categories: data exposure, model transparency, operational dependence, and regulatory impact. Each requires specific inquiry during due diligence and ongoing monitoring throughout the relationship.
- Regulatory responsibility for vendor AI does not transfer to the vendor. The institution remains accountable for AI-driven outcomes that affect members, regardless of where the model resides or who built it.
- AI due diligence must be integrated into existing vendor management workflows rather than operated as a parallel process. The four risk categories should be layered into standard questionnaires, contract reviews, and periodic assessments.
- Due diligence leverage is highest before the contract is signed. The vendor's response to AI-specific due diligence questions, including its willingness to provide documentation and accept contractual protections, is itself a meaningful risk indicator.

Questions for Leadership

1. Have we inventoried our current vendor portfolio for AI capabilities, and do we know which vendors are processing member data through AI systems?
2. Does our standard vendor questionnaire include AI-specific questions covering data exposure, model transparency, operational dependence, and regulatory impact?
3. For vendors with AI capabilities touching member financial data, do our contracts include explicit provisions governing data handling, model change notification, and audit rights?
4. Are our AI-enabled vendor relationships reflected in our business continuity planning, including documented manual fallback procedures?
5. Has our compliance officer reviewed the regulatory impact of our highest-risk vendor AI systems, including fair lending and adverse action notice implications?

Further Reading

- NCUA Letter 21-CU-08: Relationships with Third Parties—National Credit Union Administration.
- FFIEC IT Examination Handbook, Third-Party Relationships Booklet—Federal Financial Institutions Examination Council.

- SR 11-7: Model Risk Management, Vendor and Third-Party Model Section—Federal Reserve Board/OCC.
- NIST AI RMF, MAP Function: AI Risk in Third-Party and Supply Chain Contexts—NIST.
- CFPB Circular 2022-03: Adverse Action Notification Requirements and the Role of Artificial Intelligence—CFPB.

PART III

Governing AI Already in Use

Chapters 7–11 govern AI systems already operating in the environment—building the inventory, managing shadow AI, governing data flows, understanding security risks, and establishing the monitoring program.

CHAPTER 7

Identifying AI Systems in the Environment

Opening Scenario

The Information Security Program Manager (ISPM) has been asked to present the institution's AI inventory to the Risk Committee. He had started the process six weeks earlier, confident that the exercise would be straightforward. The credit union was not a large institution. Just how many AI systems might exist?

The first week, he surveyed IT. They identified four systems: the fraud detection module in the core platform, the AI-assisted member onboarding tool, the vendor had introduced in the last update cycle, a chatbot that the digital banking team had piloted briefly before shelving it, and the smart routing feature in the member services platform. Four systems. He felt good about that number.

He was, as it turned out, off by ten.

In the second week, he sent a brief survey to department heads asking a single question: Does your team use any tools, applications, or vendor features that use AI or machine learning to automate tasks, analyze information, or generate content? The responses came back across five business days. When he finished reading them, his four-system inventory had grown to fourteen.

B. A. Salas, *AI Risk Management for Financial Institutions*,
https://doi.org/10.1007/979-8-8688-3353-3_7

Lending used an AI-powered document analysis tool to extract data from loan applications; a feature added by their document management vendor that nobody had flagged to IT. Marketing used two generative AI platforms: one for copy drafting and one for social media image generation. The finance team had recently started using an AI-assisted forecasting module in their budget planning software. HR used an AI screening tool integrated into their applicant tracking system. The collections department had a vendor-provided AI tool that analyzed account behavioral patterns and recommended outreach timing for delinquent accounts. Member services had four staff members using a generative AI tool informally for drafting correspondence; a different tool than the one marketing used, and again not disclosed to IT.

Fourteen systems. Ten of them were unknown to the security program before the survey. Six of them were touching member data in ways that had never been reviewed against GLBA requirements. Two of them informed decisions, lending document analysis and collections behavioral scoring, that the institution had never risk-assessed.

The ISPM presented all fourteen to the Risk Committee. The room was quieter than usual when he finished. The committee chair asks a question that would set the direction for the next quarter's work: "How do we ensure this list stays current?"

The Risk Problem

The AI inventory is the foundational artifact of the governance program. Every other governance activity: risk assessment, vendor due diligence, monitoring, policy enforcement, and incident response, depends on the inventory being accurate and current. A governance program built on an incomplete inventory is not a governance program. It is a partial response to a problem whose full scope is unknown.

The discovery problem described in the opening scenario is not unusual. It reflects two structural realities of how AI arrives in organizational environments. First, channels such as vendor feature updates, departmental software purchases made under operational budgets, and individual staff adoption of freely available tools allow AI capabilities to proliferate, bypassing IT and security programs. Second, the people closest to these tools, the staff using them daily, rarely recognize them as AI systems that require governance attention. They experience them as useful features, not as risk management objects.

The risk problem is therefore not primarily technical. It is organizational. Building an accurate AI inventory requires a discovery process that reaches across department boundaries, a communication strategy that makes the concept of AI governance legible to non-technical staff, and a maintenance process that keeps the inventory current as the environment evolves. None of those are technical problems. They are program management problems.

Why It Matters to Credit Unions

For credit unions operating with small security teams, the temptation to treat the AI inventory as a one-time project is understandable. Building it is effort-intensive. Maintaining it requires ongoing attention from an already stretched program. But an inventory that is accurate today and out of date in six months is not a governance asset; it is a false confidence risk. The institution believes it knows what is in its environment when it does not.

NCUA examiners reviewing AI governance will ask to see the inventory. They will also ask questions designed to test whether the inventory is complete: Are there tools used by staff in their daily workflows that are not on this list? How was the inventory built, and how is it maintained? When was it last updated? An institution that can answer those questions with documented, credible processes is in a fundamentally different examination posture than one that presents a static list without a maintenance story.

The inventory also serves an internal communication function that matters beyond compliance. When leadership can see the full picture of AI use in the institution, including the informal and departmental tools that have accumulated outside IT visibility, the conversation about AI governance shifts from abstract to concrete. The risk is no longer theoretical. It is specific, named, and actionable. That shift is often what creates the organizational will to resource the governance program properly.

Governance and Risk Considerations

Building and maintaining an accurate AI inventory requires a structured approach of three phases: initial discovery, classification and documentation, and ongoing maintenance. Each phase has distinct methods and governance considerations.

Phase 1: Initial Discovery

Initial discovery should cast as wide a net as possible. The goal is to surface every AI system in the environment, including those that arrived outside formal procurement channels. Three complementary discovery methods, used together, produce the most complete initial inventory.

IT and security review examine known systems: vendor platforms in the technology register, applications in the software asset inventory, and any systems that IT has direct visibility into. This method reliably surfaces formally purchased and IT-managed systems. It routinely misses departmental tools and staff-adopted applications.

The departmental survey reaches the people closest to the work. A brief, accessible survey sent to department heads and team leads, asking whether their team uses any tools that automate tasks, analyze data, generate content, or make recommendations, surfaces the informal AI use that IT reviews cannot reach. The survey should be designed for non-technical respondents: it should not use technical AI terminology that staff may not associate with the tools they use. Describing capabilities rather than asking about "AI" produces more accurate responses.

Vendor portfolio review examines each active vendor relationship for AI capabilities, using the process established in Chapter 6. This method surfaces embedded AI in platforms that were bought for non-AI purposes; this category is most likely to be missed by both IT review and departmental survey.

Phase 2: Classification and Documentation

Once discovered, each system must be classified and documented in the inventory record. The AI Risk Classification Model from Chapter 4 provides the classification framework. The inventory record for each system should capture a standard set of fields that supports both governance decisions and examination review.

AI Inventory: Core Data Fields System name and vendor • Classification level (1–4) • Primary function and use case

Business unit owner • IT/security owner • Member data involved (yes/no, type)

Deployment status (active/pilot/inactive) • Date added to inventory

Date of last risk assessment • Current risk disposition • Open remediation items

Vendor contract status • AI-specific contract provisions in place (yes/no)

Notes on the discovery method and any disclosure gaps identified

---

The inventory record should be maintained in a format that supports regular review and update; a spreadsheet, a GRC platform, or a dedicated risk register are all appropriate. The format matters less than the discipline of keeping it current. We should ensure that the ISPM, the risk manager, the compliance officer, and the Risk Committee can access whatever system is used for their review.

Classification is not always straightforward. Some systems span multiple levels depending on how they are used. A generative AI tool used to draft internal process documentation is Level 1. The same tool used to draft member adverse action notices is at a minimum Level 2 and potentially Level 3, depending on how the content is generated and reviewed. The inventory should document the actual use case, not the theoretical capability of the tool, and the classification should reflect that use.

Phase 3: Ongoing Maintenance

An AI inventory that is built once and not maintained is worse than no inventory; it creates a false sense of completeness while the actual environment continues to evolve. Maintenance requires both periodic refresh and continuous intake mechanisms.

Periodic refresh should be conducted at least annually and should replicate the initial discovery process in abbreviated form: a departmental check-in survey, a vendor portfolio review for changes, and an IT review of any new systems added since the last refresh. The refresh should be documented as a governance activity with a record of what was reviewed, what changed, and what was added or removed from the inventory.

Continuous intake requires that the discovery process is embedded in existing workflows rather than dependent on periodic campaigns. Three integration points are most effective: the IT change management process, which should flag any new software deployment or vendor update for AI capability assessment; the vendor management process, which should trigger an inventory update whenever a vendor relationship changes; and the staff acceptable use policy, which should establish a reporting obligation for staff who begin using AI tools so that informal adoption is surfaced promptly rather than discovered during the next annual survey.

Handling Discovered but Unapproved Systems

Initial discoveries frequently surface AI systems that are in active use but were never formally reviewed or approved. The governance response to these systems requires judgment. An immediate prohibition on all unapproved AI tools is operationally disruptive and, in environments where AI has proliferated widely, practically unenforceable. A blanket acceptance of all discovered systems without review is a governance abdication.

The proportionate response is a structured triage: classify each discovered system, conduct a risk assessment calibrated to its classification level, and make a documented governance decision about whether use should continue, be modified, or be discontinued. Systems that are actively being used and delivering operational value at Level 1 or Level 2 with no member data exposure are likely approvable with appropriate policy coverage. Systems at Level 3 or Level 4 that were deployed without review require immediate assessment and potentially interim controls pending a full evaluation. The triage process should be time-bound and documented.

Implementation Steps

1. Launch a structured initial discovery process using all three methods: IT and security review, departmental surveys, and vendor portfolio review. Do not assume any single method will produce a complete picture. Budget two to four weeks for the initial discovery phase, depending on the size of your vendor portfolio and department structure.

2. Design the departmental survey for non-technical respondents. Describe AI capabilities in plain language, such as "tools that automatically sort or route information," "software that generates written content," "features that score or rank options based on historical patterns," rather than asking staff to identify "AI systems." The quality of survey responses is directly proportional to how accessible the questions are.

3. Build the inventory in a format that supports governance review. Include all core data fields. Make the classification level and risk disposition visible at a glance. The inventory should function as a working governance document, not an archive.

4. Establish a triage process for systems discovered through the initial inventory that were not previously reviewed. Prioritize by classification level. Document the triage decisions and the governance body that reviewed them. Treat the triage as the first round of formal risk assessment for these systems.

5. Embed inventory maintenance into existing workflows. Update the IT change management checklist to include an AI capability question for new deployments. Add an inventory update step to the vendor management annual review. Include an AI disclosure obligation in the staff's acceptable use policy. The inventory stays current when its maintenance is a byproduct of existing processes rather than a separate recurring project.

Important Points

- The AI inventory is the foundational artifact of the governance program. Every other governance activity depends on it being accurate and current.
- Initial discovery requires three complementary methods: IT and security review, departmental surveys, and vendor portfolio review. No single method surfaces the complete picture.
- The departmental survey is the most important discovery method for informal and staff-adopted AI use. It must be designed for non-technical respondents to produce reliable results.
- Inventory maintenance requires both periodic refresh and continuous intake mechanisms embedded in existing workflows. A static inventory built once is a governance liability, not a governance asset.
- Unapproved systems discovered through inventory should be triaged by classification level and given documented governance decisions; not blanket prohibited or blanket accepted.

Questions for Leadership

1. Have we conducted a structured AI discovery process using IT review, departmental survey, and vendor portfolio review, or does our current inventory rely on a single discovery method?
2. Does our AI inventory include the classification level, member data exposure status, risk disposition, and open remediation items for every identified system?
3. How is the inventory maintained between formal review cycles, and is that maintenance embedded in existing change management and vendor management workflows?
4. Have all AI systems, discovered through the initial inventory that were not previously reviewed, received a documented governance decision about continued use?
5. Could we present our AI inventory to an NCUA examiner today and explain with confidence how it was built, how it is maintained, and why it is complete?

Further Reading

- NIST AI RMF, MAP Function: AI System Inventory and Categorization—National Institute of Standards and Technology.

- FFIEC IT Examination Handbook, Management Booklet: Technology Asset Management—Federal Financial Institutions Examination Council.
- NCUA Letter 22-CU-02: Technology and Cybersecurity Supervisory Priorities—National Credit Union Administration.
- ISO/IEC 42001:2023, Clause 6: AI System Inventory and Context of Use—International Organization for Standardization.
- CISA AI Security Incident Collaboration Playbook: Inventory Guidance—Cybersecurity and Infrastructure Security Agency.

CHAPTER 8

Managing Shadow AI

Opening Scenario

It started with a help desk ticket. A member services representative had noticed that responses generated by the AI drafting tool she used had begun to include language about products the credit union did not offer. She had been using the tool for four months to draft member correspondence and had found it reliable until recently. She submitted the ticket not as a security concern but as a practical problem: the tool was producing incorrect content, and she wanted to know if IT could fix it.

The ISPM pulled the ticket during his morning review and paused. He had no record of this tool. It was not in the AI inventory. It had not gone through the evaluation process. It was not covered by any acceptable use policy or vendor agreement. A staff member had been using it for four months to communicate with members, and the institution had been unaware of its existence until a content error surfaced in a help desk queue.

He asked the representative a few questions. She had found the tool through a colleague. That colleague had found it through a LinkedIn post about productivity tools for financial services professionals. At least six people on the member services team were using it. Two of them had been pasting member account details into the prompts to personalize responses. None of them had any idea that this was a problem. They had done what any reasonable person does when they find something useful:

B. A. Salas, *AI Risk Management for Financial Institutions*,
https://doi.org/10.1007/979-8-8688-3353-3_8

shared it with a colleague, who shared it with another colleague, until it had quietly become a team-wide workflow in approximately the time it takes a security policy to get approved.

From their perspective, the tool made their jobs easier and produced better correspondence than they could draft as quickly on their own.

The ISPM's first instinct was frustration. His second instinct, the most useful one, was curiosity. How had six people adopted the same tool with no one flagging it? What had the institution communicated about AI use that made this seem acceptable? What had not been communicated that left the gap open?

The answer, when he examined it honestly, was that the institution had communicated almost nothing. There was no AI acceptable use policy. Staff lacked direction concerning permissible tools. There was no channel for staff to ask whether a tool had been approved. The gap was not a failure of staff judgment. It was a failure of institutional communication. The staff had not ignored the policy. They had operated in the absence of one.

That distinction mattered enormously to how the ISPM responded.

The Risk Problem

Shadow AI is the organizational equivalent of the inventory gap described in Chapter 7, but with an important distinction. Vendor-embedded AI arrives through institutional channels, even if it is not well disclosed. Shadow AI arrives through individual human behavior: staff members who discover useful tools, adopt them to solve immediate problems, and integrate them into their workflows without institutional awareness or approval.

The risk profile of shadow AI is distinct from formally deployed AI in two ways. First, shadow AI is, by definition, ungoverned. There is no vendor contract, no risk assessment, no acceptable use policy, no data handling review, and no monitoring. The institution has no visibility of what data is being processed, kept, or transmitted. It has no recourse if the tool behaves unexpectedly. It cannot show to examiners that the tool has been reviewed, because it has not been.

Second, shadow AI concentrates on operational workflows where staff are under productivity pressure and where the tools deliver immediate, tangible value. Member correspondence, document drafting, data analysis, customer communication personalization; these are exactly the workflows where member data is most likely to be involved and where the consequences of improper data handling are most significant. Shadow AI does not accumulate in low-stakes corners of the institution. It accumulates where the work is.

The challenge of governance is that prohibition alone does not solve the shadow AI problem. Staff adopt these tools because they are useful, freely available, and frictionless to access. An institution that responds to shadow AI discovery with blanket prohibition and disciplinary threats will drive the behavior underground rather than eliminate it. The tools will continue to be used; they will simply become invisible again. The governance response must address both the risk and the underlying conditions that produced the behavior.

Why It Matters to Credit Unions

Credit unions operate in a trust environment. The cooperative model depends on members believing that their financial information is handled with care and discretion. A shadow AI incident, member data is processed through an unapproved third-party AI tool, kept by the vendor, used to train a model, or exposed in a breach, is not just a regulatory event. It is a member trust event. The institution's response to that event, and the governance story it can tell about how the incident occurred and what it is doing to prevent recurrence, determines how much trust damage it sustains.

For small security teams, shadow AI also represents a resource allocation problem. Every unmanaged tool in the environment is a potential incident. Every incident requires response resources that small teams do not have in surplus. Proactive shadow AI governance, building the policies, communication, and culture that surface informal AI use before it becomes an incident, is a more efficient use of program resources than reactive incident management after the fact.

There is also a staff dimension that credit unions, with their community-oriented culture, should take seriously. The staff members using shadow AI tools are not malicious actors. They are people trying to do their jobs well. A governance response that treats them as policy violators rather than as participants in a gap the institution created will damage the trust relationship between the security program and the staff it depends on for cooperation. That damage has program consequences that extend well beyond the shadow AI issue itself.

Governance and Risk Considerations

Effective shadow AI governance operates across four dimensions: detection, response, policy, and culture. Each dimension addresses a different aspect of the problem, and all four must be active for the governance response to be durable.

Detection: Finding what is there

The departmental survey process described in Chapter 7 is the primary detection mechanism for shadow AI. But surveys are periodic. Between survey cycles, shadow AI adoption continues. The institution needs continuous detection mechanisms that do not depend on staff self-disclosure.

Technical detection methods include DNS and web proxy log review for traffic to known AI platforms, endpoint monitoring for AI application installations, and email and collaboration platform scanning for AI-generated content signatures where those capabilities exist within the security toolset. These methods have significant coverage limitations that practitioners should not underestimate: most widely used generative AI tools—ChatGPT, Claude, Gemini, Copilot—are browser-based applications accessed over HTTPS, and their traffic is often indistinguishable from ordinary web browsing without full Transport Layer Security (TLS) inspection, which few small credit unions have deployed. Personal devices are entirely outside institutional visibility. In practice, technical detection reliably surfaces a minority of shadow AI activity; non-technical detection channels carry the heavier governance load.

Non-technical detection methods are often more reliable in practice. Help desk tickets that reference unfamiliar tools, as in the opening scenario, are a detection signal. Manager observations during workflow reviews, peer disclosures during team meetings, and new employee onboarding conversations that reveal prior workplace AI habits are all channels through which shadow AI surfaces without formal detection infrastructure. Building awareness of these channels into the security program means that detection is not entirely dependent on technical capability.

Response: What to Do When It Is Found

The response to a discovered shadow AI instance should be proportionate to the risk it presents and constructive in its orientation toward the staff involved. A tiered response framework based on the classification level and data exposure profile of the tool is more consistent and defensible than ad hoc case-by-case decisions.

For Level 1 tools with no member data exposure, the appropriate response is typically documentation and policy coverage: add the tool to the inventory, conduct a lightweight risk assessment, issue guidance to the team about acceptable use parameters, and include the tool in the next vendor review cycle if it involves a commercial provider. No immediate discontinuation is required unless specific concerns emerge from the assessment.

For Level 2 tools or any tool where member data has been processed, the response should include an immediate data handling review: what data was processed, when, through what tool, and under what vendor terms? If the vendor's data handling terms are incompatible with GLBA or if member data was kept without authorization, a data incident assessment is warranted. A tools use should be suspended until a formal evaluation can be completed. The staff involved should be engaged constructively; their knowledge of how the tool was used and what data was involved is essential to the assessment.

For Level 3 or Level 4, shadow IT systems discovered using AI, which inform on member decisions that were deployed with no governance review, the response is more urgent. Operations should review any decisions affected by the tool's outputs, immediately start a formal risk assessment and brief leadership. These situations are rare but represent the highest potential for member harm and regulatory exposure.

Policy: Creating the Framework for Acceptable Use

A policy that does not exist cannot be violated, and its absence is the most common condition that allows shadow AI to accumulate. The AI acceptable use policy is the foundational document that gives staff the guidance they need to make appropriate decisions and gives the institution the policy basis it needs to respond when those decisions fall outside acceptable boundaries.

An effective AI acceptable use policy for credit union staff should address five core elements: what AI tools are approved for use and under what conditions; what data categories may and may not be processed through AI tools; how staff should request evaluation of a tool they want to use; how staff should report an AI tool they already use that may not have been approved; and what the consequences are for deliberate, knowing misuse of AI tools in violation of policy.

AI Acceptable Use Policy: Core Elements

1. Approved tools list—what is currently sanctioned and at what data sensitivity level
2. Data handling restrictions—what member data categories may not be processed through external AI tools without explicit approval
3. Evaluation request process—how staff request review of a tool they want to use
4. Disclosure obligation—how staff report tools currently in use that may not be approved
5. Consequence framework—what happens for deliberate policy violations (distinguished from good-faith use in the absence of guidance)

The policy should be written in accessible language, not security program jargon. Its purpose is to guide staff behavior, not to show regulatory sophistication. A policy that staff can read, understand, and apply to their daily decisions is more valuable than a comprehensive document that no one reads past the first paragraph.

Culture: Building Voluntary Disclosure

The most durable shadow AI governance mechanism is a culture in which staff are comfortable disclosing the AI tools they use, confident that disclosure will be met with a constructive response rather than immediate prohibition or disciplinary action. That culture does not emerge from policy alone. It is built through the institution's demonstrated pattern of response to early disclosure.

When a staff member discloses an AI tool they have been using informally and the response is a helpful conversation about how to use it appropriately, rather than a lecture about policy violation, the probability of future disclosure increases—both for that individual and for others who observe the exchange. When the response is punitive or dismissive, the probability of future disclosure decreases, and shadow AI goes further underground.

The ISPM and security team play an active role in culture-building by being accessible, visible, and constructive in their engagement with AI-related questions. Lunch-and-learn sessions about AI governance, clear communication channels for AI tool questions, and regular updates to staff about the approved tools list—these are culture investments that reduce the governance burden over time by increasing the volume of voluntary disclosure and reducing the volume of shadow AI that accumulates between detection cycles.

Implementation Steps

1. Draft and publish an AI acceptable use policy covering the five core elements above. If no policy currently exists, treat this as the highest-priority policy deliverable in the AI governance program. A brief, clear, accessible policy published promptly is more valuable than a comprehensive policy that

takes six months to develop. You can refine it over time; you cannot govern behavior that has not been addressed by any policy.

2. Establish a formal AI tool evaluation request process. Staff should know how to ask whether a tool is approved, and the process should have a defined response timeline. A request process that takes weeks to produce an answer incentivizes staff to adopt tools first and ask later, or not at all. Aim for a first response within five business days for Level 1 and Level 2 requests.

3. Review technical detection capabilities in your current security toolset. Determine what visibility you have into web traffic, endpoint applications, and cloud service usage. Document the gaps. You do not need to close all gaps immediately, but you should know what you can and cannot see so that your detection posture is understood rather than assumed.

4. Conduct a constructive retrospective on any shadow AI instances discovered during the initial inventory. Engage the staff involved in a learning-oriented conversation: How did they find the tool? What problem were they solving? What would have made it easier to use an approved alternative? The answers inform both policy and culture improvements.

5. Communicate the AI acceptable use policy through channels that reach staff directly, such as all-staff emails, team meetings, and manager briefings, and provide a simple reference guide that translates

policy requirements into practical daily guidance. Follow up with a brief awareness session within thirty days of policy publication.

Important Points

- Shadow AI accumulates in high-productivity, high-data-sensitivity workflows; exactly where the governance stakes are highest. It is not a peripheral risk.
- Prohibition alone does not solve the shadow AI problem. Without addressing the conditions that produce it, the absence of policy, the absence of approved alternatives, absence of a disclosure channel, prohibition drives the behavior underground rather than eliminating it.
- Response to discovered shadow AI should be proportionate and constructive. Staff using tools in the absence of guidance are in a different governance category than staff deliberately circumventing known policy requirements.
- The AI acceptable use policy is the foundational document for shadow AI governance. Its absence is the most common condition that allows shadow AI to accumulate unchecked.
- Culture is the most durable governance mechanism. An institution where staff feel comfortable disclosing AI tools they use has a fundamentally lower shadow AI risk profile than one where disclosure is associated with disciplinary consequences.

Questions for Leadership

1. Do we have a published AI-acceptable use policy that staff can access, understand, and apply to their daily decisions about AI tool use?
2. Is there a defined process for staff to request evaluation of an AI tool they want to use, and does that process have a response timeline that discourages informal adoption?
3. For shadow AI instances discovered during the AI inventory process, have we conducted a data handling review to assess whether member data was processed through unapproved tools?
4. Does our response to shadow AI discovery reflect the distinction between good faith use in a policy vacuum and deliberate circumvention of known requirements?
5. Are we investing in the cultural conditions, accessibility, visibility, and constructive response to disclosure that encourage staff to surface AI tool use proactively rather than waiting for it to be discovered?

Further Reading

- NIST AI RMF, GOVERN Function: Organizational Practices for Responsible AI Use—National Institute of Standards and Technology.

- GLBA Safeguards Rule, 16 CFR Part 314: Information Security Program Requirements—Federal Trade Commission.
- FFIEC IT Examination Handbook, Management Booklet: Information Security Culture and Awareness—FFIEC.
- NCUA Letter 20-CU-02: Cybersecurity and Information Security Program Requirements—National Credit Union Administration.
- CISA Guidance on Generative AI in the Workplace: Shadow IT Considerations—Cybersecurity and Infrastructure Security Agency.

CHAPTER 9

AI Data Governance

Opening Scenario

The compliance officer had a question that seemed simple on the surface. A member had submitted a written inquiry asking whether the credit union used any automated systems to make decisions about their account, and if so, what information those systems used. The member had read a news article about AI in banking and wanted to understand their rights.

The compliance officer brought the question to the ISPM. Together, they worked through it. The credit union's fraud detection module used behavioral transaction data, account history, and device metadata. The lending decision support tool used credit bureau data, income documentation, and the member's account relationship history. The collections outreach tool used delinquency history, payment pattern data, and contact response rates. Across three AI systems, the institution was processing eight distinct categories of member data, routing it through vendor AI infrastructure, and using the outputs to make or inform decisions that directly affected members.

The ISPM could answer the members' questions about what data was used. He lacked confidence in responding to the second part of the inquiry: vendor data retention duration. Was it used to train or improve the vendor's models? Was it shared with sub-processors? Could a member request its deletion, and if so, what happened to the modeled outputs derived from data that were subsequently deleted?

B. A. Salas, *AI Risk Management for Financial Institutions*,
https://doi.org/10.1007/979-8-8688-3353-3_9

He pulled the three vendor contracts. One addressed data retention explicitly and prohibited model training on customer data. One was silent on retention and included a broad license clause that arguably permitted model improvement use. And one had been auto renewed without legal review and contained terms that had not been evaluated against the institution's current data governance standards.

The compliance officer drafted a response to the member that answered what could be answered and flagged the gaps that could not be answered. The ISPM opened three vendor conversations. The experience produced a data governance gap assessment that became the foundation for the institution's AI data governance work plan.

The member's questions were simple. The answer revealed significant complexity. That complexity had been present in the institution's AI systems for months before anyone thought to ask.

The Risk Problem

AI systems are data systems. Every AI system in the institution's environment is consuming data, processing it, producing outputs from it, and in many cases, keeping it or using it in ways that extend beyond the immediate transaction. The data governance obligations that apply to that data classification, access control, retention, disposal, and breach notification apply regardless of whether the data is being processed by a human analyst, a traditional software system, or an AI model.

The risk problem specific to AI data governance is that AI systems often obscure the data lifecycle in ways that traditional systems do not. When a loan officer reviews a credit application, the data flow is visible: the officer accesses specific fields, makes a decision, and the record is kept according to the institution's document retention schedule. When an AI model processes the same application, the data flow is less visible: the model may ingest dozens of data points, weigh them in ways the institution cannot inspect, produce an output score, and retain a data representation of the application in a vendor's infrastructure under terms the institution may not have reviewed carefully.

That opacity creates specific governance risks: the institution may not know what data its AI systems are actually using; it may not know how long vendor AI systems keep member data; it may not know whether that data is being used beyond its original purpose; and it may not be able to fulfill member rights requests or breach notification obligations because it lacks the data map needed to do so. AI data governance is the discipline of closing those gaps.

Why It Matters to Credit Unions

GLBA Safeguards Rule obligations apply to member financial information wherever it is processed, including in vendor AI systems. The institution's information security program must extend to third-party data handling, which means the institution must know how its AI vendors handle member data and must have contractual and monitoring mechanisms to enforce standards.

Beyond GLBA, the data governance stakes for credit unions are member relational as well as regulatory. Members trust the institution with financial information that is among the most sensitive data they generate. That information flowing into AI systems, being retained, potentially reused for model training, potentially shared with sub-processors the member has never heard of, is a breach of the implicit covenant the cooperative model creates, even if it does not constitute a legal violation. AI data governance is an expression of that covenant in operational form.

State privacy laws are also an emerging consideration. Several states have enacted consumer privacy legislation that supplements federal requirements, and some of those laws include provisions affecting how automated decision systems use personal data. Credit unions operating in multiple states or serving members who have moved must know their AI data governance obligations may include state-level requirements that exceed the federal baseline.

Governance and Risk Considerations

AI data governance requires a structured approach across four areas: data classification and mapping, data handling standards, vendor data accountability, and member rights and transparency. Each area addresses a distinct aspect of the data lifecycle as it flows through AI systems.

Data Classification and Mapping

Effective AI data governance begins with knowing what data flows into each AI system. A data flow map for each AI system in the inventory should document the data categories consumed by the system, the source of that data within the institution, where it is transmitted for processing, how long it is retained by the vendor, and whether it is used for any purpose beyond the immediate transaction.

Most credit unions already have data classification frameworks that categorize member data by sensitivity level. AI data governance extends that framework into the AI system context: for each classification level, what AI processing is permissible, under what vendor accountability standards, and with what monitoring requirements? A member's account balance is classified at a different sensitivity level than their identity document images; the AI systems that process each should be governed accordingly.

The data flow map is the foundational document for AI data governance in the same way the AI inventory is the foundational document for AI risk management. Neither the risk assessment nor the vendor due diligence process can function well without knowing what data each system actually uses. Building the data flow map for each AI system should be a parallel activity to the classification and documentation phase of the inventory process.

Data Handling Standards for AI Systems

Data handling standards for AI systems should address the full data lifecycle: collection, processing, storage, use, sharing, and disposal. For each stage, the standard should specify what is permissible, what is prohibited, and what vendor accountability mechanisms are required.

Collection standards should specify which data categories may be provided to AI systems and which may not be without explicit governance review and approval. Sensitive categories, member identity documents, biometric data, health-related financial data, and detailed behavioral profiles should require elevated approval thresholds before being fed into AI systems, particularly vendor AI, where the institution has limited visibility into downstream processing.

Processing standards should address the purpose limitation principle: AI systems should not use member data collected for one purpose or for a materially different purpose without member notice and, where required, consent. A fraud detection system that uses transaction data for anomaly detection is using that data for the purpose for which it was collected. A model that uses the same transaction data to build a behavioral profile used for targeted marketing is using it for a different purpose, one that requires different governance treatment.

Retention and disposal standards should specify maximum retention periods for member data processed by AI systems, including data held by vendors, and should require vendor contractual commitments to honor disposal requests within defined time frames. These standards must account for the complexity of AI data retention: a model that has been trained on member data retains a representation of that data in its weights even after the raw data is deleted, which creates obligations and limitations that differ from traditional data disposal.

Vendor Data Accountability

Vendor data accountability mechanisms translate the institution's data handling standards into enforceable vendor obligations. The contractual provisions identified in Chapter 6, data handling terms, model training restrictions, sub-processor disclosure, and audit rights, are the primary accountability tools. In the AI data governance context, those provisions must be specific enough to govern the data lifecycle as it actually occurs within the vendor's AI infrastructure.

Monitoring vendor data handling is the ongoing accountability complement to contractual provisions. Periodic vendor assessments should include AI-specific data governance questions: has the vendor's data handling practice changed since the last review? Have sub-processors changed? Have the vendor's model training practices or data retention policies been updated? Vendor attestations covering AI data handling, included as part of the annual vendor review cycle, create a documented accountability record that supports both governance oversight and examination evidence.

AI Data Lifecycle: Key Governance Questions by Stage Collection: What data categories enter this AI system? Is the collection restricted to essentials?

Processing: Is the data used only for the purpose it was collected? Who performs the processing?

Storage: Where is data stored? For how long? Under what security controls?

Use: Is data used to train or improve vendor models? Is that permitted by the contract?

Sharing: Are sub-processors involved? Are they disclosed and contractually bound?

Disposal: How is data deleted? What is the vendor's commitment to disposal timelines?

Member Rights and Transparency

Credit union members have rights regarding their financial data, and some of those rights intersect directly with AI data governance. Adverse action notice requirements under ECOA and FCRA require that members receive meaningful explanations when AI systems contribute to adverse credit decisions. The ability to provide those explanations depends on the institution's understanding of the AI system's decision logic to translate it into actionable notice language.

More broadly, the institution should be able to answer a member who asks: What data do you use to make decisions about my account, and how is it processed? The question, like the opening scenario, is not hypothetical. It is being asked more frequently as public awareness of AI in financial services grows. An institution that can answer it clearly demonstrates both technical competence and the kind of member-first transparency the cooperative model demands from those who hold its members' financial lives in trust.

Transparency does not require the institution to disclose proprietary vendor model details it does not have access to. It requires honest communication about what data is used, for what purpose, and what rights the member has regarding that data. Building that transparency capability requires the data flow maps, the vendor accountability terms, and the governance infrastructure described in this chapter. It cannot be improvised in response to a member's inquiry. It must be built in advance. Chapter 17 addresses how that transparency capability connects to the broader responsible AI commitments that define the credit union's relationship with its members.

Implementation Steps

1. Build data flow maps for each AI system in the inventory. For each system, document the data categories consumed, the source of that data, where it is processed and stored, the vendor's retention period, and whether it is used for model training. Start with Level 3 and Level 4 systems where member data exposure and decision impact are highest. Complete Level 1 and Level 2 systems in the subsequent review cycle.

2. Review current vendor contracts against your data handling standards. Identify contracts that are silent on AI data retention, that include broad license language that may permit model training use, or that have not been reviewed since AI capabilities were added. Prioritize these for renegotiation or addendum at the next renewal opportunity.

3. Establish a purpose limitation standard for AI data use. Document which data categories may be provided to AI systems and for what purposes. Make this standard explicit in your AI data governance policy so that decisions about new AI data flows have a documented framework to reference rather than being made on an ad hoc basis.

4. Develop a response framework for member data rights requests that accounts for AI data processing. The framework should specify how the institution responds to requests for information about automated decision-making, how it fulfills adverse

action notice obligations for AI-assisted credit decisions, and how it handles requests for data deletion where AI model training is involved.

5. Include AI data governance questions in the annual vendor review cycle. Add a standing section to the periodic vendor assessment that covers data handling changes, sub-processor updates, model training practice changes, and data retention policy updates. Document vendor responses and flag material changes for the Risk Committee's review.

Important Points

- AI systems are data systems. Every AI governance obligation is downstream of knowing what data each system uses, how it is processed, and where it goes after the transaction is complete.
- The data flow map is the foundational AI data governance artifact. It must be built for every AI system in the inventory and kept current as vendor practices and institutional use cases evolve.
- GLBA Safeguards Rule obligations extend fully to vendor AI data processing. The contracts, monitoring, and periodic accountability reviews described in this chapter are the operational form of that responsibility.
- Purpose limitation, which involves using member data solely for its intended collection purpose, is a governance standard applicable to AI systems. Data handling standards and vendor contracts must explicitly address this.

- Member transparency about AI data use is both a regulatory obligation and a cooperative value. The institution must be able to answer member questions about automated decision-making clearly, specifically, and without improvisation.

Questions for Leadership

1. Do we have a data flow map for each AI system in our inventory that documents the data categories consumed, processing location, retention period, and model training use?
2. Have our vendor contracts for AI-enabled systems been reviewed against our data handling standards, including provisions on retention, model training, and sub-processor disclosure?
3. Do we have an established purpose limitation standard that defines which data categories may be provided to AI systems and for what purposes?
4. Can we answer a member's inquiry about automated decision-making clearly and specifically, including what data is used, how it is processed, and what rights the member has?
5. Are AI data governance questions, retention changes, training practice updates, and sub-processor changes included in our annual vendor review cycle?

Further Reading

- GLBA Safeguards Rule, 16 CFR Part 314: Information Security Program and Third-Party Oversight—FTC.
- CFPB Circular 2022-03: Adverse Action Notification Requirements and Explainability in AI—CFPB.
- NIST AI RMF, MAP Function: Data Provenance and Governance in AI Systems—NIST.
- NCUA Letter 21-CU-08: Third-Party Relationships and Data Handling Obligations—NCUA.
- FFIEC IT Examination Handbook, Information Security Booklet: Data Classification and Lifecycle Management—FFIEC.

CHAPTER 10

Security Risks in AI Systems

Opening Scenario

The fraud alert came through on a Thursday afternoon. A member had reported a series of transactions she had not allowed; small purchases at unfamiliar retailers, each just below the threshold that would have triggered the credit union's fraud detection system automatically. The pattern was deliberate: someone had tested the AI fraud model's detection boundary and was exploiting it systematically.

The ISPM pulled the transaction logs and confirmed what the member had described. Seventeen transactions over six days, each between forty and sixty dollars, each at a different merchant, each processed and cleared without a fraud flag. The model had performed exactly as designed. The problem was that someone outside the institution had learned enough about how the model performed to design an attack around its blind spot.

He escalated to the fraud team and the vendor. The vendor confirmed that the behavior was consistent with a known vulnerability class in behavioral fraud models: adversarial probing, in which an attacker systematically tests transaction parameters to map the detection boundary, then operates just inside it. The vendor had published a model

B. A. Salas, *AI Risk Management for Financial Institutions*,
https://doi.org/10.1007/979-8-8688-3353-3_10

update addressing the specific pattern three weeks earlier. The credit union had not yet applied it. The gap between the patch release and its application was the window the attacker had used.

The incident was contained. The member was made whole. The patch was applied. But the ISPM spent the following week documenting what the incident had revealed about the institution's security posture regarding its AI systems: there was no defined process for monitoring AI vendor security updates separate from general platform patching. There was no threat model for the specific attack surfaces that AI systems introduced. There was no staff awareness that AI systems could be targeted differently from conventional software.

The fraud model had not been hacked. It had been studied. The distinction mattered because the countermeasure was not a firewall rule or an access control change. It was a governance process: staying current on AI-specific threat intelligence and vendor model updates with security implications. That was a different kind of security work than the team had been doing, and it required a different kind of program attention.

The Risk Problem

AI systems introduce security risks that are distinct from the risks of conventional software. Traditional security threats, unauthorized access, data exfiltration, denial of service, and malware apply to AI systems as they do to any technology asset. But AI systems also carry a set of threat vectors that are specific to how machine learning models function: threats that exploit the statistical nature of model behavior rather than the vulnerabilities in the underlying code.

These AI-specific threats are not yet widely understood outside of specialized security research communities, which means they are frequently absent from threat models, security assessments, and vendor questionnaires at most financial institutions. The security program that addresses conventional software vulnerabilities comprehensively but does not account for AI-specific attack surfaces has a gap that is growing as AI becomes more central to institutional operations.

For credit unions operating primarily as AI consumers rather than developers, the AI security threat landscape is filtered through the vendor relationship. The institution does not have direct access to the model infrastructure it would need to mount a technical defense against most AI-specific attacks. What it has is the ability to understand the threat landscape, ask vendors the right security questions, stay current on AI security developments, and build the detection and response capabilities needed to identify when an AI system is being exploited, even if the exploitation occurs at the model level rather than the infrastructure level.

Why It Matters to Credit Unions

Financial institutions are high-value targets for AI-specific attacks because AI systems at credit unions are often directly connected to financial decisions: fraud detection, lending, and account management. Attacks that successfully manipulate these systems produce financial outcomes for the attacker: fraudulent transactions approved, legitimate fraud suppressed, and lending decisions manipulated. The financial incentive to understand and exploit AI model vulnerabilities in the financial services sector is high and growing.

Credit unions also face the security risk asymmetry that characterizes the vendor AI relationship. The attacker who studies a vendor's fraud model to find its detection boundary may be studying a model deployed across dozens or hundreds of credit unions that use the same platform. A successful attack methodology developed against one institution works across the entire customer base. The vendor's security response, model updates, detection improvements, and threat intelligence are both the most important security control and one that the institution does not directly control. Vendor accountability for AI security is not a nice-to-have; it is a structural dependency.

From an examination standpoint, AI security is increasingly within scope for NCUA technology reviews. Examiners are not yet applying AI-specific security examination modules at most institutions, but the question of whether the institution's information security program accounts for the specific risks introduced by AI systems is a reasonable examiner inquiry, given the regulatory direction of travel. An institution that can demonstrate awareness of AI-specific threats and documented controls to address them is in a meaningfully stronger position than one that treats AI security as synonymous with general IT security.

Governance and Risk Considerations

Understanding the AI security threat landscape requires familiarity with the principal attack categories that are specific to machine learning systems. Six threat categories are most relevant to the credit union AI consumer environment.

Adversarial Attacks

Adversarial attacks involve deliberately crafted inputs designed to cause an AI model to produce incorrect outputs. In the financial services context, the most practically relevant form is the boundary probing described in the opening scenario: systematically testing model behavior to identify the thresholds at which detection or adverse classification occurs, then operating just inside those thresholds to evade detection.

Defense against adversarial attacks is primarily a vendor's responsibility, including model robustness improvements, adversarial training, and anomaly detection at the model level. The institution's role is to ensure the vendor is actively monitoring for adversarial activity, that model updates addressing known adversarial patterns are applied promptly, and that the institution's own transaction monitoring can detect behavioral patterns consistent with adversarial probing even when individual transactions do not trigger model alerts.

Prompt Injection

Prompt injection is the most immediately relevant AI security threat for institutions using large language model (LLM)-based tools: generative AI platforms, AI-assisted drafting tools, AI chatbots for member services, and any system that accepts natural language input and passes it to an underlying AI model. In a prompt injection attack, malicious instructions are embedded in content that the AI system processes, causing it to take actions or produce outputs that its operators did not intend.

In the credit union context, prompt injection risks are most acute in member-facing AI applications, chatbots, automated correspondence tools, or AI-assisted forms processing, where external parties can craft inputs that reach the underlying AI system. A member service chatbot that processes member-submitted text could be manipulated through carefully crafted messages to produce misleading responses, disclose information it should not, or take actions outside its intended scope.

Controls for prompt injection include input validation and sanitization before content reaches the AI model, strict output filtering and review for member-facing AI applications, clear separation between the AI system's processing context and user-provided content, and staff awareness of the threat in systems where staff interact with AI-generated outputs that may have been influenced by external inputs.

Model Poisoning

Model poisoning occurs when an attacker can influence the data used to train an AI model, causing the model to learn incorrect patterns or to behave in predictable ways under specific conditions that the attacker can later exploit. For credit unions consuming vendor AI, model poisoning risk is primarily a vendor-side threat: an attacker who can influence the data used to train or retrain a vendor's model affects every institution using that model.

The institution's primary defense against model poisoning in vendor AI is accountability: requiring vendors to document their training data provenance and validation processes, asking about data quality controls and anomaly detection in training pipelines, and staying current on vendor communications about model behavior anomalies that might indicate training data integrity issues. An institution that receives a vendor notification about anomalous model behavior and can quickly assess whether that behavior affects its operational use cases is better positioned to respond than one without that monitoring infrastructure.

Data Extraction and Model Inversion

Data extraction attacks attempt to recover training data or sensitive information from an AI model through careful querying of its outputs. Model inversion attacks use model outputs to reconstruct approximations of the input data on which the model was trained. Both attack categories are relevant when an AI model has been trained on member data, either by the institution or by a vendor using institutional data.

The practical defense for credit unions is the vendor data governance accountability established in Chapter 9: contractual prohibitions on training vendor models on member data without consent, combined with monitoring of model output patterns for anomalies that might show extraction activity. For internally managed AI systems, if any exist in the institution's environment, access controls on model query interfaces and output logging are the primary technical controls.

Supply Chain Attacks on AI Components

AI systems frequently depend on open-source model components, third-party AI libraries, and cloud-based model infrastructure. Supply chain attacks targeting these dependencies can compromise AI system behavior without directly attacking the institution's own infrastructure. A malicious component introduced into an open-source AI library used by a vendor's platform affects every customer of that platform, with no direct attack on any individual institution.

Credit unions cannot audit their vendors' entire AI software supply chains, but they can ask vendors about their software composition security practices, their use of vetted and monitored AI components, and their process for responding to supply chain security disclosures. Vendor security questionnaires should include AI software supply chain questions, and vendor responses should be part of the periodic security assessment record.

AI-Enhanced Threats Against the Institution

The last category is distinct from the others: rather than attacks on AI systems, these are attacks against institutions that use AI as a tool. AI-generated phishing content, deepfake audio and video used in social engineering, and AI-assisted reconnaissance that tailors attacks to specific institutional vulnerabilities are all active and growing threat vectors.

AI-enhanced social engineering deserves particular attention in the credit union environment, given the community and relationship-oriented culture that characterizes these institutions. Staff who are accustomed to personalized, relationship-based member interactions may be more susceptible to highly personalized AI-generated phishing or voice cloning attacks that leverage publicly available information to create convincing impersonations. Security awareness training must be updated to address AI-enhanced threat scenarios specifically, not just the traditional phishing and vishing patterns most programs currently cover.

AI Security Threat Summary for Credit Union Environments Adversarial attacks: boundary probing to evade fraud and detection models

Prompt injection: malicious inputs manipulating LLM-based member-facing applications

Model poisoning: training data manipulation affecting vendor model behavior

Data extraction/model inversion: recovering member data from model outputs

Supply chain attacks: compromised AI components in vendor platforms

AI-enhanced threats: deepfakes, AI-generated phishing, and targeted social engineering

---

Security Control Extensions for AI Systems

Addressing AI-specific security risks does not require building a separate security program. It requires extending the existing security control framework to account for AI-specific threat vectors. The extension points map naturally onto existing control domains.

Vulnerability management should include AI model update monitoring as a distinct track alongside conventional software patching. Vendor AI model security updates, particularly those addressing adversarial patterns, prompt injection vulnerabilities, or training data integrity issues, should be tracked, assessed for applicability, and applied on a defined timeline. The absence of this track means that AI-specific security improvements go unapplied while the institution believes its patching program is comprehensive.

Threat intelligence should include AI-specific sources: NIST AI security guidance, MITRE ATLAS (the AI threat landscape framework), vendor security bulletins for AI platforms, and industry sharing through FS-ISAC channels, where AI threat intelligence is increasingly distributed. Staff who monitor threat intelligence should have an awareness of AI-specific threat categories so that relevant intelligence is recognized and acted on rather than filtered out as unfamiliar.

Security awareness training should be updated to include AI-enhanced threat scenarios. Staff needs to understand that AI-generated phishing, voice cloning, and deepfake video are active threat vectors, not theoretical future risks. Training scenarios that include realistic AI-enhanced attacks, rather than the obvious, poorly written phishing examples that characterize most traditional programs, produce more effective awareness.

Incident response procedures should include AI-specific scenarios: adversarial attack detection, prompt injection in member-facing applications, anomalous AI model behavior, and AI-enhanced social engineering incidents. Each of these scenarios has response characteristics that differ from conventional incident types, and teams should not encounter them for the first time during an active incident.

Implementation Steps

1. Add AI-specific threat categories to your institution's threat model. For each AI system in the inventory, identify which of the six threat categories above are applicable based on the system's function and deployment context. Document the applicable threats in the risk assessment record for each system. This does not require deep technical threat modeling; it requires applying the threat categories to what you know about how each system works and who interacts with it.

2. Establish an AI model update monitoring process separate from general software patching. Work with AI-enabled vendors to ensure that security-relevant model updates are communicated clearly and that the institution has a defined process for assessing and applying them. Add AI model update status to the vulnerability management program's tracking scope.

3. Add AI security questions to vendor security assessments. Ask vendors about adversarial attack monitoring, prompt injection controls in LLM-based products, training data integrity processes, software supply chain security practices, and their process for communicating AI security incidents to customers. Document responses and flag gaps for follow-up.

4. Update security awareness training to include AI-enhanced threat scenarios. Develop at least two training scenarios that involve AI-generated phishing or voice cloning attacks. Brief staff on the existence and growing sophistication of these threats. Update the training program annually as the AI threat landscape evolves.

5. Add AI-specific incident scenarios to incident response procedures. Develop tabletop scenarios covering adversarial fraud model manipulation, prompt injection in a member-facing application, and AI-enhanced social engineering. Conduct at least one tabletop exercise per year that includes an AI-specific scenario so that response teams are familiar with these situations before encountering them in practice.

Important Points

- AI systems introduce security threats that are distinct from conventional software vulnerabilities. A security program that does not account for AI-specific attack surfaces has a gap that grows as AI becomes more operationally central.
- The six principal AI security threat categories for credit union environments are adversarial attacks, prompt injections, model poisoning, data extraction and model inversion, supply chain attacks, and AI-enhanced threats against the institution.

- For credit unions consuming vendor AI, most AI-specific security defenses are vendor-side responsibilities. The institution's role is accountability: ensuring vendors maintain appropriate defenses, communicating security updates promptly, and staying current on AI-specific threat intelligence.
- AI security does not require a separate program. It requires extending existing control domains, vulnerability management, threat intelligence, security awareness, and incident response to include AI-specific threat vectors and response scenarios.
- AI-enhanced social engineering, deepfakes, voice cloning, and AI-generated phishing are active and growing threats that security awareness programs must address with realistic, current scenarios rather than outdated training materials.

Questions for Leadership

1. Does our threat model include AI-specific attack categories, and have we assessed which of those categories apply to each AI system in our inventory?
2. Do we have a defined process for monitoring and applying AI model security updates from vendors, distinct from our general software patching program?
3. Do our vendor security assessments include questions about adversarial attack monitoring, prompt injection controls, training data integrity, and AI security incident communication?

4. Has our security awareness training been updated to include AI-enhanced threat scenarios, deepfakes, voice cloning, and AI-generated phishing that reflect the current threat landscape?
5. Do our incident response procedures include AI-specific scenarios, and has the team conducted a tabletop exercise that tests response to an AI-related security incident?

Further Reading

- NIST AI RMF, MANAGE Function: AI-Specific Security Controls and Incident Response—NIST.
- MITRE ATLAS: Adversarial Threat Landscape for Artificial Intelligence Systems—MITRE Corporation.
- NIST SP 1270: Towards a Standard for Identifying and Managing Bias in Artificial Intelligence—NIST.
- FS-ISAC AI and Machine Learning Threat Intelligence Resources—Financial Services Information Sharing and Analysis Center.
- CISA Guidance on AI Cybersecurity: Secure by Design Principles for AI Systems—CISA.

CHAPTER 11

Monitoring and Oversight of AI Systems

Opening Scenario

Eight months after the institution's fraud detection model had been deployed, the ISPM noticed something in the monthly exception report. Fraud losses had increased modestly over the prior quarter; not dramatically, not enough to trigger a formal incident, but a directional shift that had not been present in the prior six months. The model's true positive rate had declined slightly. False negatives, transactions that the model cleared that turned out to be fraudulent, were up.

He brought it to the vendor's account team. Their initial response was that the numbers were within normal performance variance. He asked for the model's baseline performance documentation from the time of deployment so he could compare. It took two weeks to get it. When he did, the comparison was clear: the model had been performing measurably below its documented baseline for approximately five months.

The vendor investigated. The explanation they eventually provided was that the model had been retrained six months earlier as part of a scheduled improvement cycle. The retraining had used a broader national

B. A. Salas, *AI Risk Management for Financial Institutions*,
https://doi.org/10.1007/979-8-8688-3353-3_11

transaction dataset that improved overall model performance across the vendor's customer base. But the credit union's membership had demographic and behavioral characteristics that differed from the national dataset in ways that the broader training had not accommodated well. The model that had been tuned to the institution's member behavior had been replaced with a model tuned to a different population, and five months of elevated fraud losses were the result.

The vendor issued a corrective model update within thirty days of the investigation. The losses were not catastrophic. But the ISPM spent considerable time afterward documenting what the incident had shown: the institution had no monitoring process that would have caught the performance degradation earlier. It had no contractual requirement for vendor notification when the model was retrained. And it had no baseline performance benchmark against which to measure ongoing behavior.

All three gaps were addressable. None of them had seemed urgent before the incident. All of them seemed urgent after that.

The Risk Problem

The governance activities covered in the preceding chapters—inventory, classification, risk assessment, vendor due diligence, data governance, security controls—are all oriented toward understanding and managing AI risk at a point in time. Monitoring is the governance activity that extends management across time. It is the mechanism through which the institution detects when the risk profile of an AI system has changed, due to model retraining, expanded use, changed member demographics, evolving threat patterns, or simple model drift, before that change accumulates into a significant governance failure.

The risk problem specific to AI monitoring is that AI systems can degrade in ways that are not visible through conventional system monitoring. A server that goes down produces an alert. A model that begins performing below its documented baseline produces fraud losses, lending errors, or member service failures that may be attributed to other causes before the model is identified as the source. AI performance degradation is often gradual, statistical, and easy to rationalize as normal variance until enough data accumulates to make the pattern undeniable.

For institutions that do not have active AI monitoring programs, this means that risk can accumulate for months before it is detected. By the time it surfaces—through an examiner's question, a member complaint pattern, or an incident like the one in the opening scenario, the exposure has already materialized. Monitoring is the governance activity that converts latent risk into visible, manageable risk before it becomes realized harm.

Why It Matters to Credit Unions

SR 11-7, the model risk management guidance that applies to financial institution AI systems, explicitly requires ongoing monitoring of model performance. The guidance establishes that model validation is not a onetime event conducted at deployment but a continuous obligation that includes periodic performance review, outcome analysis, and reassessment when model behavior changes. An institution that deploys an AI system, conducts a pre-deployment evaluation, and considers the governance obligation fulfilled has not met the standard SR 11-7 establishes.

For credit unions, the monitoring obligation has a member dimension that extends beyond regulatory compliance. AI systems that inform decisions about members, lending, fraud, and collections are producing outcomes that affect real people. A fraud model that degrades silently allows fraudulent transactions to harm members. A lending model that drifts from its validated behavior may produce decisions that are inconsistent, unfair, or discriminatory in ways the institution cannot detect without monitoring. Member harm from unmonitored AI system degradation is not a regulatory abstraction. It is a direct failure of the institution's responsibility to its members.

The resource reality for small teams is that comprehensive AI monitoring cannot require the same investment of time and attention as the systems being monitored. Monitoring must be proportionate, systematic, and integrated into existing oversight workflows. A monitoring program that requires the ISPM to manually review AI performance metrics weekly for every system in the inventory will not be sustained. A monitoring program that produces a monthly exception report, reviewed at the Risk Committee, is sustainable and defensible.

Governance and Risk Considerations

Effective AI monitoring operates across three domains: performance monitoring, behavioral monitoring, and governance monitoring. Each domain addresses a distinct dimension of AI system oversight and requires different data sources, review cadences, and escalation criteria.

Performance Monitoring

Performance monitoring tracks whether an AI system is producing outputs consistent with its documented baseline. For quantitative models, fraud detection, credit scoring, and behavioral analytics, performance metrics are statistical: true positive and false positive rates, precision and recall, score distributions, and decision threshold adherence. For generative AI systems, drafting tools, chatbots, and document analysis, performance monitoring is more qualitative: output accuracy, relevance, consistency, and the absence of harmful or incorrect content.

Establishing a performance baseline at deployment is a prerequisite for meaningful performance monitoring. Without a documented baseline, the institution cannot identify deviations. The baseline should include the key performance metrics documented by the vendor at validation, the institution-specific performance observations from the first sixty to ninety days of operational use, and the acceptable performance range within which the system is expected to operate. Monitoring then compares current performance against that baseline on a defined schedule.

Performance monitoring data should come from both vendor-provided reporting and institution-side outcome tracking. Vendor-provided dashboards and performance reports are the primary source for model-level metrics. Institution-side outcome tracking, fraud loss trends, loan performance by channel, and member complaint patterns provide the operational signal that connects model behavior to real outcomes. Both data sources are needed; neither alone is sufficient.

Behavioral Monitoring

Behavioral monitoring tracks whether an AI system is being used in ways consistent with its intended purpose and governance approvals. Performance monitoring asks: Is the system working correctly? Behavioral monitoring asks: Is the system being used correctly?

Staff usage patterns are the primary subject of behavioral monitoring for most credit union AI deployments. Are loan officers overriding the AI recommendation system at unusually high or low rates? Are member service staff bypassing the AI triage system for certain inquiry types? Are staff using AI drafting tools to process data categories that were not included in the approved use case? Anomalies in usage patterns are often the earliest signal that something in the operational use of an AI system has drifted from its governance approvals.

Behavioral monitoring also applies to member-facing AI systems. Are member interactions with AI chatbots producing escalation rates that are higher than expected? Are AI-assisted correspondence outputs generating a higher-than-normal rate of member follow-up questions or complaints? These patterns may indicate that the system's outputs are not meeting member needs in ways that performance metrics alone would not reveal.

Behavioral monitoring does not require surveillance-level visibility into staff activities. It requires periodic review of operational metrics that are already being collected: loan officer decision rates, member service escalation rates, and output review logs for AI drafting systems. The monitoring value is in reviewing those metrics with AI governance intent, looking for patterns that suggest usage drift, rather than collecting new data.

Governance Monitoring

Governance monitoring tracks whether the institutional governance structures around AI systems remain current and effective. It answers questions that performance and behavioral monitoring do not: Are the risk assessments for AI systems being conducted on schedule? Are open remediation items from prior assessments being closed? Have vendor contracts been reviewed since AI capabilities were added? Is the AI inventory current? Has the board received AI governance briefings on the defined schedule?

Governance monitoring is essentially the audit function applied to the AI governance program itself. It ensures that the program is operating as designed rather than atrophying between formal review cycles. For small teams, governance monitoring is often the most easily neglected dimension because it does not produce operational alerts or financial signals; it produces program health indicators that only matter when an examiner asks or when a governance failure becomes an incident.

A simple governance monitoring checklist, reviewed monthly by the ISPM and quarterly by the Risk Committee, is sufficient for most credit unions. The checklist should cover assessment currency for each system, remediation tracking status, inventory update date, vendor review schedule adherence, and board briefing currency. Items that fall out of compliance with defined schedules should be escalated rather than silently deferred.

Escalation Criteria and Response

Monitoring produces value only when it is connected to defined escalation criteria and response processes. An exception report that is produced but never reviewed, or that surfaces anomalies without a defined response path, does not reduce risk. It creates the appearance of oversight without the substance.

Escalation criteria should be defined for each AI system at the time of risk assessment and documented in the risk assessment record. For a fraud detection model, an escalation trigger might be a true positive rate that falls over ten percent below the documented baseline for two consecutive months. For a lending decision support system, an escalation trigger might be a demographic performance disparity that exceeds defined thresholds in quarterly outcome analysis. For a generative AI tool, an escalation trigger might be a member complaint rate on AI-assisted correspondence that doubles the baseline rate.

When an escalation trigger is met, the response should follow a defined path: immediate notification to the ISPM, review of recent vendor communications for related model updates or known issues, assessment of whether affected members have experienced harm, and Risk Committee notification if the issue cannot be resolved within a defined time frame. The response path should be documented so that it does not depend on an individual judgment about how serious the anomaly is when it occurs.

AI Monitoring Framework Summary Performance monitoring: Is the system producing output consistent with its baseline?

- Frequency: Monthly for Level 3–4, quarterly for Level 1–2
- Sources: Vendor performance reports + institution-side outcome tracking

Behavioral monitoring: Is the system being used consistently with its governance ap**provals?**

- Frequency: Quarterly review of usage pattern metrics
- Sources: Staff usage logs, member interaction metrics, output review records

Governance monitoring: Is the governance program around AI systems operating as d**esigned?**

- Frequency: Monthly ISPM checklist, quarterly Risk Committee review
- Sources: Assessment schedule, remediation log, inventory currency, board briefing record

Connecting Monitoring to the Risk Assessment Cycle

Monitoring and risk assessment are complementary rather than redundant. Risk assessment provides the point-in-time risk picture and establishes the monitoring parameters. Monitoring produces a continuous data stream that informs the next risk assessment. When monitoring identifies performance degradation or behavioral drift, it triggers an out-of-cycle risk assessment rather than waiting for the next scheduled review. When risk assessment identifies additional risks or revised risk ratings, it updates the monitoring parameters to reflect the changed risk profile.

This feedback loop is the operational heart of Layer 3 of the AI Governance Pyramid. Without it, risk management is episodic and retrospective. With it, risk management is continuous and prospective, identifying emerging issues before they become governance failures rather than documenting failures after they have already affected members or attracted examiner attention.

Implementation Steps

1. Establish performance baselines for each Level 1 and Level 2 AI system currently in operation. If baseline documentation was not captured at deployment, request it from the vendor and supplement it with the last ninety days of performance data. Document the baseline in the risk assessment record for each system. Without a baseline, performance monitoring cannot produce meaningful signals.

2. Design a monthly AI monitoring report that merges performance, behavioral, and governance indicators for all systems in the inventory. The report does not need to be elaborate; a structured summary that flags exceptions against defined thresholds is more valuable than a detailed analytical document that no one reads. Assign the report to a standing agenda slot in the Risk Committee meeting.

3. Define escalation criteria for each Level 3 and Level 4 system and document them in the risk assessment record. The criteria should be specific, named metrics, quantified thresholds, and defined measurement periods, rather than qualitative judgments. Specific criteria produce consistent escalation decisions; qualitative judgments produce inconsistent ones that depend on who is reviewing the report in any given month.

4. Include vendor notification requirements for model retraining in upcoming contract renewals. The opening scenario describes the consequence of the absence of this requirement. Vendors should be contractually obligated to notify the institution at least thirty days before a scheduled model retraining event, with documentation of the retraining scope and expected performance impact. Out-of-cycle retraining triggered by security or regulatory requirements should require notification within five business days.

5. Conduct a governance monitoring review annually as a standalone program health assessment. Review every AI system in the inventory against the governance monitoring checklist: assessment currency, remediation status, vendor review schedule, inventory currency, and board briefing schedule. Document the findings and present them to the Risk Committee. The annual governance monitoring review is the program's self-assessment mechanism and its most direct examination preparation activity

Important Points

- Monitoring extends AI risk management across time. Without it, governance activities conducted at deployment become stale as systems evolve, drift, and are retrained without institutional awareness.
- AI performance degradation is often gradual and statistical, not sudden and alertable. It accumulates silently until it reaches a threshold visible in operational outcomes: fraud losses, lending errors, and member complaints. Monitoring is the mechanism that surfaces it earlier.
- Effective AI monitoring operates across three domains: performance monitoring (is the system working correctly?), behavioral monitoring (is it being used correctly?), and governance monitoring (is the governance program operating as designed?).
- Monitoring produces value only when connected to defined escalation criteria and documented response processes. An exception report without a response path is theater, not governance.
- Monitoring and risk assessment form a feedback loop that is the operational core of the AI risk management function. Monitoring triggers out-of-cycle assessments; assessments update monitoring parameters. Together, they make risk management continuous rather than episodic.

Questions for Leadership

1. Do we have documented performance baselines for each Level 3 and Level 4 AI system in operation, and are we actively comparing current performance against those baselines?
2. Does the Risk Committee receive a regular AI monitoring report, and does that report flag exceptions against defined performance and behavioral thresholds?
3. Have we defined specific escalation criteria for each high-risk AI system—named metrics, quantified thresholds, and defined measurement periods—rather than relying on qualitative judgment about when to escalate?
4. Do our vendor contracts for AI systems include notification requirements for model retraining, and are those requirements specific enough to give the institution meaningful advance notice?
5. When did we last conduct a governance monitoring review that assessed whether the AI governance program itself is operating as designed, and were the findings presented to the Risk Committee?

Further Reading

- SR 11-7: Supervisory Guidance on Model Risk Management, Ongoing Monitoring and Outcomes Analysis—Federal Reserve Board/OCC.

- NIST AI RMF, MANAGE Function: Ongoing Monitoring and Incident Response for AI Systems—NIST.
- FFIEC IT Examination Handbook, Audit Booklet: Continuous Monitoring and Exception Reporting—FFIEC.
- ISO/IEC 42001:2023, Clause 9: Performance Evaluation and Continuous Improvement of AI Systems—ISO.
- NCUA Examiner's Guide: Technology Risk Management and Ongoing Oversight Expectations—NCUA.

PART IV

Building an AI Risk Program

Chapters 12–15 construct the formal governance infrastructure: the framework, the committee, the control model, and incident response. The operational work of Parts II and III is given institutional form here.

CHAPTER 12

Designing an AI Governance Framework

Opening Scenario

Twelve months after the initial AI inventory had surfaced fourteen systems across the institution, the ISPM sat down to take stock. The program had come a long way. There was a current inventory. Risk assessments existed for every Level 3 and Level 4 system. The vendor questionnaire had been updated. An acceptable use policy was published. A monthly monitoring report went to the Risk Committee. The gaps that had been invisible a year ago were now documented, tracked, and being closed.

What the program still lacked was architecture. The activities that had been built were real and valuable, but they had been built in response to immediate needs rather than against a deliberate design. There was no policy that formally established the AI governance program. There was no defined governance committee with standing authority over AI risk decisions. No documented accountability structure connected the ISPM's operational work to executive oversight and board awareness. The program functioned in practice. Explaining its coherent structure remained impossible for now.

B. A. Salas, *AI Risk Management for Financial Institutions*,
https://doi.org/10.1007/979-8-8688-3353-3_12

That gap mattered for two reasons. The first was examination readiness. A collection of artifacts would not satisfy an NCUA examiner reviewing AI governance without a governing framework. The artifacts needed to exist within a documented structure that assigned accountability, established policy, and connected operational governance to institutional leadership.

The second reason was sustainability. Programs built on individual effort rather than institutional structure are fragile. If the ISPM left, or the risk manager changed, or the CEO turned over, the program's continuity would depend on institutional memory rather than documented design. A governance framework converted the program from a personal project into an institutional capability.

The ISPM pulled out the AI Governance Committee Structure model he had developed during the early months of the program and began mapping the institution's current state against it. Formally, the committee had not yet been established, but the key individuals were already informally involved. The policy did not yet exist as a standalone document, but its content was distributed across several existing documents. The accountability matrix had never been written, but the informal expectations were reasonably well understood.

The framework existed in practice. The work ahead was to make it legible; to convert informal practice into a documented structure that the institution could stand behind, communicate to examiners, and sustain across personnel changes.

The Risk Problem

The risk problem at Layer 4 of the AI Governance Pyramid is structural rather than operational. The activities addressing operational risks, ungoverned systems, poor vendor oversight, unmonitored performance degradation, and shadow AI accumulation were built into Parts II and

III. Structural risk arises because those activities lack a formal governance framework for permission, institutional accountability, and long-term continuity.

A governance program without a framework depends on the judgment and attention of the individuals who happen to be running it. When those individuals are engaged and resourced, the program functions. The program atrophies when individuals are not engaged and resourced, when turnover occurs, when competing priorities crowd out AI governance, and when institutional memory is not transferred. The framework is what makes the program institutional rather than personal.

The specific structural risks that an AI governance framework addresses are accountability gaps, policy vacuums, and oversight disconnects. Accountability gaps occur when AI risk decisions are made without a defined authority structure; when it is unclear who can approve a Level 4 deployment, who owns remediation for a high-risk finding, or who is responsible for presenting AI risk to the board. Policy vacuums occur when governance expectations exist in practice but not in writing, making them unenforceable and unverifiable by examiners. Oversight disconnects occur when operational AI governance activities are not connected to institutional leadership in a way that produces informed decision-making at the executive and board levels.

Why It Matters to Credit Unions

For credit unions, the governance framework serves three audiences simultaneously. For examiners, it provides the documented structure they look for when assessing whether an institution takes AI governance seriously: a named policy, a defined committee, a documented accountability structure, and evidence that leadership is engaged. For the board, it provides the institutional commitment they need to exercise meaningful oversight rather than receiving ad hoc AI updates without a program context to place them in. And for the security and risk team, it provides the institutional authority that makes AI governance decisions stick; the difference between an ISPM recommendation that is politely noted and one that carries formal governance weight.

A credit union with a handful of AI systems does not need the governance infrastructure of a major bank. It needs a framework that is appropriately scaled: a policy that establishes the program, a committee that is small enough to function efficiently, and an accountability structure that reflects the institution's actual organizational complexity. A governance framework that is too elaborate for the institution it serves will not be maintained. The design goal is the minimum viable structure that is genuinely defensible.

Governance and Risk Considerations

The AI governance framework has four components: the AI governance policy, the AI Governance Committee Structure, the accountability matrix, and the governance calendar. Each component addresses a distinct structural need, and together they make up the Layer 4 architecture of the AI Governance Pyramid.

Component 1: The AI Governance Policy

The AI governance policy is the foundational document that formally establishes the institution's AI governance program. It defines the program's scope, objectives, and governing principles; establishes the authority of the AI Governance Committee; references the subsidiary policies and standards that govern specific aspects of AI use; and assigns top-level accountability for AI governance to named roles.

The policy does not need to be lengthy. A well-designed AI governance policy for a credit union can be structured in five sections: purpose and scope, governing principles, program structure and accountability, subsidiary policy references, and review and amendment requirements. The content of each section draws on the frameworks and standards established throughout Parts II and III: the classification model, the risk assessment methodology, the vendor evaluation framework, the data governance standards, and the monitoring requirements. The policy brings those elements together under a single governing document rather than leaving them as disconnected artifacts.

The frequency of policy reviews should be defined in the document itself. Annual reviews are standard; out-of-cycle reviews should be triggered by material changes in the institution's AI environment, significant regulatory guidance updates, or AI governance incidents that reveal policy gaps. The review record should be maintained as evidence of program currency.

Component 2: The AI Governance Committee Structure

The AI Governance Committee Structure is the fourth proprietary framework introduced in this book. It defines the membership, authority, and responsibilities of the governance body that provides institutional oversight of AI risk. For credit unions, the committee is not a new organizational entity built from scratch—it is a defined configuration of existing roles that are already carrying AI-related responsibilities, given formal standing and a clear charter.

AI GOVERNANCE COMMITTEE STRUCTURE

CORE MEMBERS	OPTIONAL MEMBERS
• Information Security — owns AI risk assessment, monitoring, and security controls • Risk Management — owns enterprise risk integration and risk appetite alignment • Compliance — owns regulatory mapping and examination interface • Technology Leadership — owns AI system deployment and vendor management • Legal (if available) — owns contract review and regulatory interpretation	• Data Governance — engaged for data classification and lifecycle decisions • Internal Audit — engaged for program assurance and examination preparation • Business Unit Representatives — engaged for use case review and operational context

COMMITTEE RESPONSIBILITIES

- Review and approve AI deployments at Level 3 and Level 4
- Review AI risk assessments and formally accept risk disposition decisions
- Approve high-risk AI use cases and conditional acceptance conditions
- Monitor AI incidents and oversee remediation progress
- Review the AI governance program's health and recommend improvements
- Prepare and deliver AI governance briefings to executive leadership and the board

Figure 12-1. *The AI Governance Committee Structure—defined membership, authority, and responsibilities*

Committee size should be calibrated to the institution's complexity. A five-person credit union executive team may make up the de facto AI governance committee with no additional formal structure required. A larger institution with distinct IT, risk, compliance, and legal functions may need a more formally constituted body with a defined chair, quorum requirements, and meeting minutes. The governance formality should match the institution's size and regulatory profile, not an idealized enterprise standard.

The meeting cadence for the AI Governance Committee should be at a minimum of quarterly, with the ability to convene on short notice for Level 4 deployment approvals, significant AI incidents, or material regulatory guidance that requires a program response. Quarterly meetings that produce documented minutes create the governance record that examiners look for when assessing board and leadership engagement with AI risk.

Component 3: The Accountability Matrix

The accountability matrix translates the committee structure into specific decision rights and responsibilities for each governance activity in the program. It answers the question that every governance program must be able to answer clearly: for any given AI governance decision or activity, who is responsible for doing it, who reviews and approves it, and who is informed of the outcome?

A practical accountability matrix for credit union AI governance should cover the following activity categories: AI system deployment approval by classification level; risk assessment ownership and review; vendor AI due diligence ownership and contract approval authority; acceptable use policy enforcement and exception approval; monitoring report production and escalation authority; incident response ownership for AI-specific incidents; board reporting preparation and delivery; and policy review and amendment authority.

For each activity, the matrix assigns three roles using a RACI-style structure: Responsible (who does the work), Accountable (who owns the outcome and has ultimate authority), and Informed (who receives the outcome for awareness). The matrix does not need to be complex. At a small credit union, many accountability cells will resolve to the same two or three individuals. Its value lies in making accountability explicit rather than assumed, so that gaps in coverage are visible and role transitions can be managed without program disruption.

Component 4: The Governance Calendar

The governance calendar operationalizes the framework by converting governance obligations into scheduled activities that are anchored to the institutional calendar. Without a calendar, governance activities compete with operational priorities and tend to be deferred. With a calendar, they are expected events that planning accommodates.

A credit union AI governance calendar should schedule the following on defined cycles: monthly AI monitoring report production and distribution; quarterly AI Governance Committee meetings with defined agenda components; semi-annual risk assessment reviews for Level 2 systems; quarterly risk assessment reviews for Level 3 and Level 4 systems; annual AI inventory refresh; annual AI governance policy review; annual board AI governance briefing; and annual AI security awareness training update. The calendar should be integrated into the institution's master compliance and governance calendar rather than maintained as a separate document.

AI Governance Framework: The Four Components

1. AI Governance Policy—establishes the program, defines scope, and assigns top-level accountability
2. AI Governance Committee Structure—defines membership, authority, and responsibilities of the formal oversight body
3. Accountability Matrix—maps every governance activity to Responsible, Accountable, and Informed roles
4. Governance Calendar—converts governance obligations into scheduled institutional activities anchored to the annual planning cycle

---

Implementation Steps

1. Draft the AI governance policy using the five-section structure above. Draw on the frameworks, standards, and procedures already built through Parts II and III: the classification model, risk assessment methodology, vendor evaluation framework, data governance standards, and monitoring requirements are all policy content that already exists. The drafting work is largely organization and formalization rather than creation from scratch.

2. Formally establish the AI Governance Committee. Identify the core members from existing roles, define the chair, establish the meeting cadence, and document the committee's authority in a charter or terms of reference that is approved by executive leadership. Announce the committee's formation to the organization so that business units know who owns AI governance decisions and how to engage with the committee.

3. Build the accountability matrix for the full set of AI governance activities. Start with the activities already in operation and document the current de facto accountability. Then review the full activity list and identify any gaps—activities for which no role currently has clear ownership. Close those gaps in the matrix before they become examination findings or governance failures.

4. Integrate AI governance activities into the institutional governance calendar. Work with the Risk Committee and executive team to ensure AI governance reviews are on the calendar as standing agenda items rather than ad hoc requests. Ensure AI governance activities remain on the calendar; their omission is unacceptable.

5. Present the completed governance framework to the Risk Committee and executive leadership for formal adoption. The presentation should position the framework as the structure within which all the AI governance work for the prior year has been operating, now formalized and documented. Formal adoption creates the institutional record of leadership engagement with AI governance that examiners will look for.

Important Points

- A governance framework converts individual AI governance activities into an institutional capability. Without it, the program is as fragile as the individuals running it.
- The four components of the AI governance framework—policy, committee structure, accountability matrix, and governance calendar—address the structural risks of accountability gaps, policy vacuums, oversight disconnects, and governance atrophy.

- The AI Governance Committee structure does not require a new organizational entity. It is a formally chartered configuration of existing roles, given defined authority and standing responsibilities for AI governance oversight.
- The accountability matrix makes governance accountability explicit rather than assumed. Its value lies in making gaps visible and role transitions manageable, not in creating complexity.
- Framework design should be calibrated to institutional complexity. The minimum viable structure that is genuinely defensible is the right target, not an idealized enterprise governance model that will not be sustained at the institution's scale.

Questions for Leadership

1. Does a formal AI governance policy exist that establishes the program, defines its scope, and assigns top-level accountability to named roles?
2. Has the AI Governance Committee been formally established with a defined charter, named membership, clear authority over AI risk decisions, and a documented meeting cadence?
3. Is there a documented accountability matrix that assigns Responsible, Accountable, and Informed roles to every significant AI governance activity?

4. Are AI governance activities integrated into the institutional governance calendar as standing, scheduled events rather than ad hoc requests that compete with operational priorities?

5. Has the governance framework been formally adopted by executive leadership, and does that adoption appear in the institutional record in a form that examiners can review?

Further Reading

- NIST AI RMF, GOVERN Function: Organizational Roles, Responsibilities, and Authorities for AI—NIST.
- ISO/IEC 42001:2023, Clause 5: Leadership and Commitment for AI Management Systems—ISO.
- FFIEC IT Examination Handbook, Management Booklet: IT Governance and Organizational Structure—FFIEC.
- NCUA Supervisory Letter: Corporate Governance and Risk Management Expectations—NCUA.
- COSO Enterprise Risk Management Framework: Governance and Culture Components—Committee of Sponsoring Organizations.

CHAPTER 13

Establishing AI Risk Oversight

Opening Scenario

The AI Governance Committee held its first formal meeting six weeks after the framework had been adopted. The ISPM had prepared an agenda, circulated pre-read materials, and structured the discussion around three standing items: program status, open risk decisions, and emerging issues. The meeting had gone well. The committee reviewed two risk assessments, approved one Level 3 deployment with conditions, and noted three monitoring exceptions for follow-up.

The second meeting had also gone well. The CFO and the compliance officer both had conflicts the same week, making rescheduling difficult, so they canceled the third meeting. The fourth had been shortened to thirty minutes because the agenda had grown beyond what the original time slot could accommodate. By the sixth meeting, two committee members were attending inconsistently, and the pre-read materials were no longer being read before the meeting.

The ISPM recognized what was happening. The committee had been established with the right people, given a clear charter, and launched with genuine institutional will. What had not been given was

B. A. Salas, *AI Risk Management for Financial Institutions*,
https://doi.org/10.1007/979-8-8688-3353-3_13

an operating model that could sustain itself against the natural entropy of busy professionals with competing priorities. The structure existed. The discipline of operating it had not yet been established.

He brought the problem to the committee chair, the Chief Risk Officer, directly. The conversation was candid. The CRO acknowledged the attendance drift and the abbreviated meetings. She asked what the committee needed to function consistently. The ISPM had come prepared with a specific answer: a fixed quarterly cadence with protected calendar time, a standing agenda template that kept meetings to sixty minutes, a defined pre-read format that could be reviewed in twenty minutes, a clear escalation protocol that distinguished between decisions requiring full committee review and operational matters the ISPM could handle independently, and a reporting template for briefing executive leadership that did not require rebuilding the narrative from scratch each quarter.

The CRO approved all five. The committee meeting that followed lasted sixty-two minutes, was fully attended, and produced three documented decisions. The operating model had been the missing piece, not the structure.

The Risk Problem

The risk problem that Chapter 13 addresses is governance atrophy: the gradual degradation of a formally established governance structure into one that exists on paper but does not function in practice. Governance atrophy is not a failure of intent. Institutions that establish AI governance committees, adopt policies, and build accountability matrices do so with genuine commitment. The atrophy occurs because the operating model that sustains those structures against organizational entropy was not built with the same care as the structures themselves.

A committee that meets inconsistently produces inconsistent oversight. Risk decisions that wait for a quorum that never assembles accumulate into a backlog that eventually gets resolved informally rather than through the governance process. Monitoring exceptions that are noted but not formally dispositioned becomes a paper record of identified issues rather than a record of managed risk. The appearance of oversight persists; the substance erodes.

For examiners, governance atrophy is visible in the documentary record. Meeting minutes that show declining attendance, agendas that grow shorter over time, risk decisions documented as "noted" rather than formally accepted or escalated, and board briefings that become less substantive over successive quarters are all signals that a governance structure is operating below its designed capacity. The examiner who reviews the full record over eighteen months sees a different picture than the one who reviews only the most recent meeting minutes.

Why It Matters to Credit Unions

Credit unions operate with governance structures that already demand significant time from a relatively small group of senior staff. The CEO, CRO, CISO, compliance officer, and technology leader who make up the AI Governance Committee are the same people running board committees, managing examinations, leading strategic planning, and handling the full spectrum of institutional operations. Adding a governance function to their portfolios requires that the function be designed for their actual capacity, not for an idealized version of it.

The operating model design principles that work for credit union AI governance are efficiency, clarity, and proportionality. Meetings should be short enough to fit into an already full calendar. Agendas should be structured enough so that preparation time is predictable. Escalation criteria should be clear enough that committee members are not called on for decisions that could be handled at a lower level. And reporting formats should be stable enough that producing the board briefing does not require a significant creative effort each quarter.

When the governance structure is designed for the people who will operate it rather than for an abstract institutional ideal, it sustains. When it is designed for a version of the institution that does not exist, one with more time, more staff, and more dedicated governance resources than the reality, it atrophies. The sustainability of AI risk oversight at a credit union is a design problem as much as it is a commitment problem.

Governance and Risk Considerations

Effective AI risk oversight requires four operational disciplines: meeting management, escalation protocols, upward reporting, and enterprise risk integration. Each discipline addresses a distinct dimension of how the governance structure functions in practice rather than on paper.

Meeting Management

AI Governance Committee meetings should be designed to produce documented decisions, not to facilitate open-ended discussion. A sixty-minute quarterly meeting with a structured agenda, pre-circulated materials, and defined decision items is more valuable than a two-hour meeting that covers the same ground through discussion without producing logical outcomes.

The standing agenda for a quarterly AI Governance Committee meeting should include five components: a program status update covering inventory changes, monitoring exceptions, and open remediation items since the last meeting; risk assessment reviews for any systems assessed since the last meeting; deployment approvals for any Level 3 or Level 4 systems pending committee approval; emerging issues requiring committee awareness or direction; and upward reporting preparation; a brief review of the content to be included in the next executive or board briefing.

Pre-read materials should be circulated at least five business days before each meeting and designed to be reviewed in twenty minutes or less. A one-page program status summary, individual risk assessment summaries for items requiring committee review, and a brief emerging issues memo are the core pre-read package. Committee members who have reviewed the pre-read arrive prepared to decide rather than to receive information, which is the difference between a productive sixty-minute meeting and an inconclusive two-hour one.

Meeting minutes should document attendance, agenda items covered, decisions made with their rationale, and action items with assigned owners and due dates. The minutes are the governance records that examiners review. They should reflect that the committee engaged substantively with AI risk rather than simply noting the ISPM's report. Questions asked, conditions imposed on approvals, escalations requested, and dissenting views noted are all elements that give the minutes the character of genuine oversight rather than pro forma documentation.

Escalation Protocol

A clear escalation protocol defines what requires full committee review and what the ISPM can handle operationally with documented notification to the committee. Without this clarity, two failure modes emerge: either every operational decision is escalated to the committee, creating an unsustainable agenda burden, or nothing is formally escalated, and the committee's role atrophies to a reporting function without decision authority.

The escalation protocol should specify the following as requiring full committee review and formal approval: new Level 3 or Level 4 AI system deployments; risk assessment findings with high or critical residual risk ratings; risk disposition decisions that involve accepting risk above the defined risk appetite; material changes to vendor AI capabilities in Level 3 or Level 4 systems; and AI-related incidents that resulted in member harm or regulatory notification. The ISPM can handle everything below these thresholds operationally, with documentation provided to the committee as an informational item at the next meeting.

Out-of-cycle escalation, convening the committee between scheduled quarterly meetings, should be reserved for situations that cannot wait for the next scheduled meeting: an active AI-related incident with significant member impact, a regulatory inquiry specifically about AI governance, or a proposed Level 4 deployment with a business-driven timeline that requires approval before the next quarterly meeting. Out-of-cycle meetings can be conducted efficiently by conference call with a narrow agenda and decisions documented in the minutes of the next formal meeting.

Upward Reporting

The AI Governance Committee's reporting obligation runs in two directions: to executive leadership on a quarterly basis and to the board annually at a minimum. Each reporting context has different audience characteristics and different content requirements.

Executive reporting should provide the risk picture needed to support resource allocation and strategic decisions. The executive AI governance report should include a summary of the current AI risk posture across the inventory, the status of open high-risk items and their remediation progress, any decisions requiring executive authority beyond the committee's delegated scope, and forward-looking issues that may require executive attention in the coming quarter. The report should be concise, two to three pages, and structured for an audience that will read it in ten minutes and act on specific items.

Board reporting should provide the oversight information the board needs to fulfill its fiduciary responsibility for AI risk without requiring board members to understand technical details. The annual board AI governance briefing should cover the institution's AI risk posture at a summary level, the status of the governance program against its design intent, any material risk items that required executive or committed escalation during the year, and the program's forward agenda for the coming year. The briefing should be structured as a presentation rather than a report, with a five-to-seven slide deck that can be delivered in twenty minutes, with time for board questions.

Quarterly AI Governance Committee: Standing Agenda

1. Program status (10 min)—inventory changes, monitoring exceptions, remediation tracking
2. Risk assessment reviews (20 min)—new assessments, updated ratings, disposition decisions
3. Deployment approvals (15 min)—Level 3/4 systems pending committee approval
4. Emerging issues (10 min)—regulatory developments, vendor notifications, new threat intelligence
5. Upward reporting review (5 min)—confirm content for the next executive or board briefing

Total: 60 minutes • Pre-read circulated 5 business days prior • Minutes within 5 days of meeting

---

Enterprise Risk Integration

AI risk governance should not operate as a standalone function disconnected from the institution's broader enterprise risk management framework. AI risk is enterprise risk: it has financial, operational, compliance, reputational, and strategic dimensions that connect directly to the risk domains the institution's ERM framework already manages. Integrating AI governance into ERM ensures AI risk is visible in the full risk picture that the board and executive leadership receive, that AI risk appetite decisions are made within the context of the institution's overall risk posture, and that AI governance resources are allocated through the same priority-setting process as other risk management investments.

In practice, ERM integration means that AI risk findings feed into the institution's risk register alongside operational, credit, and compliance risks; that the AI governance program's resource requirements are included in the annual risk management budget process; that AI-related incidents trigger the enterprise incident management process rather than a parallel AI-specific response; and that the AI Governance Committee's reporting is included in the consolidated risk reporting that the board receives rather than presented as a separate, standalone briefing that competes for board attention with other risk topics.

For credit unions where the ERM framework is relatively lean, integration may be as simple as adding an AI risk section to the existing Risk Committee agenda and risk register. The goal is connectivity, not architectural complexity. AI risk that exists in its own governance silo is at risk of being under-resourced, under-escalated, and under-visible to the leadership and board oversight that makes governance consequential.

Implementation Steps

1. Establish the standing agenda template and pre-read format for the AI Governance Committee meetings. Design the agenda to fit sixty minutes and the pre-read to be reviewable in twenty. Pilot the format for two consecutive meetings and refine based on committee feedback before treating it as fixed. A meeting format that the committee finds efficient is one they will protect on their calendars.

2. Document the escalation protocol in writing and distribute it to committee members and relevant operational staff. The protocol should be specific enough that it answers the question, "Does this need to go to the committee?" without requiring a phone call to the ISPM. Include it as an appendix to the AI governance policy or the committee charter.
3. Develop a quarterly executive reporting template that can be completed from the committee meeting minutes in under an hour. The template should have stable sections: risk posture summary, open items, decisions made, forward agenda, so that the reporting effort is additive rather than reconstructive each quarter. Review the first two reports with the CRO to calibrate the content to executive expectations.
4. Develop the annual board AI governance briefing deck as a reusable template. Build it once with stable structural sections and a design that reflects the institution's board presentation standards. Each year's briefing updates the content within the structure rather than rebuilding the deck. The consistency signals program maturity; the efficiency makes the annual briefing sustainable.
5. Map AI risk categories into the institution's existing risk register and ERM reporting framework. Work with the risk management function to ensure that AI risk items are captured in the format that feeds consolidated risk reporting. This integration step converts AI governance from a separate program

into a visible component of the institution's full risk picture; the position it needs to occupy to be resourced and prioritized appropriately.

Important Points

- Governance atrophy, the gradual erosion of a formally established structure into one that exists on paper but not in practice, is the primary risk addressed by this chapter. It is a design problem as much as a commitment problem.
- The operating model that sustains the governance structure: meeting management, escalation protocols, upward reporting formats, and ERM integration requires the same deliberate design as the structure itself.
- Governance committee meetings should be designed to produce documented decisions, not open-ended discussions. Sixty minutes, a structured agenda, pre-circulated materials, and clear decision items are the operating parameters that make meetings sustainable.
- The escalation protocol defines what requires full committee review versus what the ISPM can handle operationally. Without this clarity, either the committee is overwhelmed with operational decisions or its authority atrophies through disuse.
- AI risk governance integrated into the institution's ERM framework is more durable, better resourced, and more visible to board oversight than AI governance operating in its own silo.

Questions for Leadership

1. Does the AI Governance Committee have a standing agenda template, a pre-read format, and a meeting cadence that committee members can realistically sustain alongside their other responsibilities?
2. Is there a documented escalation protocol that defines what requires full committee review versus what the ISPM can handle operationally, and is that protocol understood by both committee members and operational staff?
3. Does executive leadership receive a quarterly AI governance report in a format that supports resource allocation and strategic decision-making without requiring significant preparation time from the ISPM?
4. Has the board received an AI governance briefing in the past twelve months, and is an annual briefing scheduled as a standing item in the board's governance calendar?
5. Is AI risk visible in the institution's enterprise risk register and consolidated risk reporting, or does it exist only in standalone AI governance documents that are separate from the full risk picture?

Further Reading

- NIST AI RMF, GOVERN Function: Oversight Mechanisms and Escalation Processes for AI Risk—NIST.

- FFIEC IT Examination Handbook, Management Booklet: Risk Reporting and Escalation to Leadership—FFIEC.
- NCUA Letter to Credit Unions: Board Oversight and Governance Responsibilities—NCUA.
- COSO ERM Framework: Risk Governance, Oversight, and Risk Appetite Integration—Committee of Sponsoring Organizations.
- ISO/IEC 42001:2023, Clause 9.3: Management Review and Governance Reporting for AI Systems—ISO.

CHAPTER 14

AI Control Models and Risk Management

Opening Scenario

The risk assessment for the lending decision support system had rated the residual risk as high. The committee reviewed it, accepted it conditionally, and assigned three remediation items: obtain the vendor's fair lending testing results, negotiate a model change notification clause into the contract renewal, and implement a quarterly outcome analysis process to track decision disparity by demographic segment. The due date for all three was ninety days out.

Sixty days later, the ISPM reviewed the remediation log. The vendor's fair lending documentation had arrived and was on file; the testing had been conducted on a national dataset and showed no statistically significant disparate impact at the national level, though the vendor had noted that institution-specific testing was not included. The contract negotiation was in progress; legal counsel submitted the proposed model notification clause, and the vendor had responded with a modified version that required thirty days' notice for scheduled retraining events but excluded emergency model updates. The outcome analysis process had not yet started.

B. A. Salas, *AI Risk Management for Financial Institutions*,
https://doi.org/10.1007/979-8-8688-3353-3_14

He documented the status of each item and thought carefully about what the remediation log was actually telling him. Two of the three controls were partially in place. The third was not yet operational. The residual risk rating of high was still accurate—the controls he had identified as necessary had not yet fully closed the gap. But the question he now needed to answer was more specific: given the controls that were in place, what was the institution's actual control coverage for the specific risks the assessment had identified, and where were the remaining gaps most acute?

He built a simple control mapping table. For each risk identified in the assessment, model opacity, fair lending exposure, change management gap, and outcome drift over time, he listed the controls that addressed it, assessed whether each control was designed appropriately and operated effectively, and identified the residual exposure for each risk after the controls were applied. The table made something visible that the remediation log alone had not: the fair lending risk had meaningful control coverage despite the limitations in the vendor's documentation. The change management gap had partial coverage. The outcome drift risk had essentially no coverage because the monitoring process had not been built.

That specificity changed the remediation priority. The outcome analysis process, the one item that had not been started, was the highest-priority remediation because it was the only control addressing the risk category with zero current coverage. The ISPM escalated it to the committee chair with a revised ninety-day plan that put it first.

The Risk Problem

The risk problem at the control layer of AI governance is the gap between control existence and control effectiveness. Most institutions that have built AI governance programs have controls in place: vendor contracts with data handling provisions, acceptable use policies, monitoring reports, and risk assessment documentation. The governance question is not whether those controls exist, but whether they actually reduce the risk they address, and by how much.

Control existence is necessary but not sufficient. A vendor contract clause that requires data handling standards is a designed control. Whether that clause is being honored by the vendor, whether the institution has a mechanism to verify compliance, and whether a violation of the clause would be detected before it caused member harm are questions about control effectiveness that the existence of the clause does not answer. A risk assessment that evaluates control effectiveness by confirming that controls are documented rather than by assessing whether they function as intended produces a systematically optimistic residual risk picture.

For AI systems specifically, control effectiveness is more difficult to assess than for conventional IT systems because many of the most important controls are vendor-side: model validation processes, training data quality controls, adversarial attack monitoring, and fair lending testing. The institution cannot directly observe these controls operating. It must assess their effectiveness through proxy indicators: documentation quality, vendor responsiveness to inquiries, contractual accountability mechanisms, and operational outcomes. That indirection requires a more deliberate control assessment methodology than most standard IT risk frameworks provide.

Why It Matters to Credit Unions

NCUA examiners assessing AI governance are not simply looking for evidence that controls exist. They are assessing whether the institution understands its own control environment well enough to know where it is protected and where it is exposed. An institution that can present a control mapping showing which risks are well covered, which are partially covered, and which have identified gaps with active remediation plans is demonstrating a materially more sophisticated governance posture than one that presents a list of controls without analysis of their effectiveness or coverage.

For credit unions with small teams, control mapping also serves as a resource allocation function. The ISPM, who knows precisely which risk categories have zero control coverage, can direct limited remediation resources to the highest-priority gaps rather than spreading effort evenly across all open items. The control model is not just a documentation artifact; it is a work prioritization tool that makes the governance program more efficient.

Control effectiveness assessment also builds an institutional knowledge base for future AI deployments. When the institution understands which control types have been effective for which risk categories in its specific operating environment, it can design better control sets for new systems rather than starting from scratch each time. That accumulated knowledge is a governance asset that compounds.

Governance and Risk Considerations

The risk assessments conducted under the framework established in Chapter 5 produce the findings that control management must address. If Chapter 5 answers "What is our residual risk?", this chapter answers "What are we doing about it?", translating assessment findings into a managed, documented control environment. Effective AI control management operates across three disciplines: control mapping by risk category, control effectiveness assessment, and control gap remediation. Together, these disciplines convert the risk assessment findings from Chapter 5 into a managed, documented control environment.

Control Mapping by Risk Category

Control mapping organizes the institution's AI controls by the risk categories they address rather than by the systems or functions they belong to. This organization reveals the coverage picture: which risk categories have multiple overlapping controls, which have single controls with no redundancy, and which have no controls at all. The AI risk categories established earlier in this book, data exposure, model opacity, operational dependence, regulatory impact, security threats, and governance gaps, provide the mapping framework.

For each risk category, the control map should identify all controls that provide coverage, classify each control as primary or compensating, and note whether the control is institution-side or vendor-side. Primary controls are those designed specifically to address the risk; compensating controls are those that reduce impact or likelihood as a secondary function. Vendor-side controls, the model validation processes, fair lending testing, and data handling standards maintained by the vendor must be distinguished from institution-side controls because they carry different assurance characteristics and different verification requirements.

Risk category	Controls in place: coverage
Data Exposure Risk: Vendor data handling clauses • GLBA-aligned contract terms • Staff Acceptable Use Policy (AUP) restrictions on member data in AI tools • Sub-processor disclosure requirements	**Strong**
Model Opacity Risk: Vendor validation documentation requests • Model limitation disclosure requirements • Staff training on output limitations • Human review requirements for Level 3 decisions	**Moderate**

(continued)

Risk category	Controls in place: coverage
Operational Dependence: Manual fallback procedure documentation • Business continuity plan AI section • Vendor SLA monitoring	**Partial**
Regulatory Impact: Compliance officer AI review • Fair lending outcome analysis • Adverse action notice process for AI decisions	**Partial**
Security Threats: AI model update monitoring • Vendor security assessment questions • Security awareness training updates • Incident response AI scenarios	**Partial**
Governance Gaps: AI governance policy • Committee oversight • Risk assessment cycle • Monitoring program • Inventory maintenance	**Strong**

Sample control map—coverage ratings reflect an illustrative program state, not a universal benchmark.

Control Effectiveness Assessment

Control effectiveness assessment asks whether each control is doing what it is designed to do. For AI governance controls, the assessment must distinguish between design effectiveness—whether the control is designed to address the risk it targets—and operational effectiveness—whether the control is functioning as designed in practice.

Design effectiveness questions are structural: Is the vendor contract clause specific enough to be enforceable? Does the acceptable use policy address the actual data handling behaviors staff exhibit, or does it describe ideal behaviors that do not match the operational reality? Is the human review requirement for Level 3 AI decisions actually implemented in the workflow, or is the AI recommendation accepted in practice without substantive review?

Operational effectiveness questions require evidence: Has the vendor actually provided the documentation the contract requires? Has the institution tested whether staff are following the acceptable use policy in practice? When did an AI recommendation last receive a substantive human challenge, and was that challenge documented? Operational effectiveness cannot be assessed from documentation alone. It requires some form of testing, sampling, or observation that produces evidence of real-world control performance.

For vendor-side controls, the primary operational effectiveness evidence is vendor attestation supplemented by outcome analysis. A vendor who attests annually that their data handling practices comply with the contract, combined with the institution's own analysis showing no anomalous data exposure incidents, provides reasonable assurance that the control is functioning. A vendor who has not provided attestation in two years, combined with gaps in the institution's vendor review record, provides much weaker assurance. The quality of the evidence matters as much as its existence.

Control Gap Remediation

Control gap remediation converts control mapping and effectiveness assessment findings into a managed action plan. The remediation plan should prioritize gaps by two dimensions: the severity of the risk category the gap leaves uncovered, and the feasibility of closing the gap within a defined time frame given available resources.

High-severity gaps with high feasibility should be addressed first: these are the remediation wins that most directly reduce risk and are achievable without exceptional resource investment. High-severity gaps with lower feasibility require a different approach: interim compensating controls that reduce exposure while the primary control is being built, with a longer-term remediation timeline and explicit risk acceptance documentation for the interim period.

Low-severity gaps across all feasibility levels should be documented and tracked, but do not require the same urgency. The governance committee should review the full remediation plan at each meeting, confirm that high-priority items are on track, and formally accept the risk associated with any gap for which remediation has been deferred beyond the original timeline. Deferred remediation that has not been formally accepted is an undocumented risk acceptance: a governance failure, even when the underlying risk is manageable.

Connecting Controls to Classification Levels

The control requirements for each AI system should be calibrated to its classification level. A Level 1 system requires a baseline control set: acceptable use policy coverage, data handling confirmation, and inclusion in the AI inventory with annual review. A Level 2 system adds vendor accountability documentation and semi-annual monitoring. A Level 3 system adds the full vendor due diligence package, fair lending or bias testing evidence, human oversight requirements, and quarterly outcome analysis. A Level 4 system adds executive approval, enhanced monitoring with defined escalation triggers, and formal incident response coverage.

This tiered control structure, the baseline for Level 1, expanding through each level to the most comprehensive for Level 4, creates a proportionate, defensible control environment that directs governance resources toward the systems that carry the most risk. It also provides a clear specification of what control gaps look like at each level: a Level 3 system without fair lending testing evidence has a defined gap, not an ambiguous one. Specificity in the control requirements makes gap identification faster and remediation prioritization clearer.

Control Requirements by Classification Level

Level 1: AUP coverage • Data handling confirmation • Inventory inclusion • Annual review

Level 2: Level 1 controls + vendor documentation • Semi-annual monitoring • Usage pattern review

Level 3: Level 2 controls + full vendor due diligence • Fair lending/bias testing evidence • Human oversight requirements • Quarterly outcome analysis • Formal risk assessment

Level 4: Level 3 controls + executive approval • Enhanced monitoring with defined escalation triggers • Formal incident response coverage • Board notification

Implementation Steps

1. Build a control map for each Level 3 and Level 4 AI system using the six risk categories as the organizing framework. For each risk category, list the controls currently in place, classify each as primary or compensating and institution-side or vendor-side, and rate coverage as strong, moderate, partial, or absent. The map does not need to be elaborate—a structured table that makes the coverage picture visible at a glance is more useful than a lengthy narrative.

2. Conduct a design effectiveness review for each control in the map. Ask: Is this control designed specifically to address the risk it targets? Is it specific enough to be enforceable? Does it address the actual risk scenario or a simplified version of it?

Document findings and flag controls with design weaknesses for redesign before assessing their operational effectiveness.

3. Gather operational effectiveness evidence for each control. For institution-side controls, identify the evidence source: policy acknowledgment records, monitoring report samples, exception logs, and staff testing results. For vendor-side controls, identify the attestation and documentation on file. Note the date of the most recent evidence for each control. Controls for which no recent operational evidence exists should be flagged as effectiveness-unknown rather than rated as effective.

4. Build a prioritized remediation plan from the control map findings. Sort gaps by risk severity and remediation feasibility. Assign ownership, due dates, and interim compensating controls for high-severity gaps that cannot be closed immediately. Present the plan to the governance committee for review and formal acceptance of any deferred remediation items.

5. Embed the control requirement tiers into the pre-deployment evaluation checklist from Chapter 4. When a new system is classified at Level 1 through Level 4, the control requirements for that level should automatically populate the evaluation checklist. This ensures that new deployments are assessed against the full control expectation from the outset rather than accumulating gaps that must be remediated after go-live.

Important Points

- Control existence is necessary but not sufficient. The governance question is not whether controls are documented but whether they reduce the risk they target, and by how much. Design effectiveness and operational effectiveness are distinct assessments requiring different evidence.
- Control mapping by risk category reveals the coverage picture: which risks are well-protected, which are partially covered, and which have no controls at all. That visibility is a prerequisite for intelligent remediation prioritization.
- Vendor-side controls require a different assurance approach than institution-side controls. They cannot be directly observed; their effectiveness must be assessed through documentation quality, vendor responsiveness, contractual accountability, and operational outcome analysis.
- The tiered control requirement structure, baseline for Level 1, expanding through each level to the most comprehensive for Level 4, creates a proportionate control environment that concentrates governance resources on the systems that carry the most risk.
- The governance committee must formally accept deferred remediation, not silently carried forward. Undocumented risk acceptance is a governance failure, even when the underlying risk is within management tolerance.

Questions for Leadership

1. Do we have a control map for each Level 3 and Level 4 AI system that identifies coverage by risk category and distinguishes between controls that are strong, partial, or absent?
2. Have we assessed the design effectiveness of our AI governance controls, whether they are specifically designed to address the risks they target, or do we rely on the existence of controls without evaluating their adequacy?
3. What is the most recent operational effectiveness evidence on file for each significant AI governance control, and are there controls for which no recent evidence exists?
4. Does our remediation plan prioritize gaps by both risk severity and feasibility, and have all deferred remediation items been formally accepted by the governance committee with documented rationale?
5. Are the control requirements for each classification level embedded in our pre-deployment evaluation process so that new AI systems enter operation with full control coverage from day one?

Further Reading

- NIST AI RMF, MANAGE Function: AI Risk Treatment and Control Effectiveness—NIST.

- SR 11-7: Supervisory Guidance on Model Risk Management, Model Controls Section—Federal Reserve Board/OCC.
- FFIEC IT Examination Handbook, Information Security Booklet: Control Frameworks and Effectiveness Testing—FFIEC.
- COSO Internal Control—Integrated Framework: Control Activities and Monitoring Components—COSO.
- ISO/IEC 42001:2023, Clause 8: Operational Controls and Performance Evaluation for AI—ISO.

CHAPTER 15

AI Incident Response

Opening Scenario

The call came from the lending department on a Friday afternoon. The loan origination system's AI-assisted underwriting module had been returning errors for two hours; not outright failures, but recommendation outputs that the loan officers described as "not making sense." Applicants with strong credit profiles were receiving low recommendation scores. Applicants with weaker profiles were receiving high ones. The pattern was consistent enough that the lending supervisor had stopped using the recommendations and was reviewing applications manually while waiting for IT to respond.

The ISPM was notified at 3:47 PM. By 4:15 PM, he had confirmed the anomaly was real, isolated it to the AI recommendation module rather than the underlying data or the loan origination platform itself, and notified the vendor. The vendor's technical team confirmed by 5:30 PM that a model configuration update deployed that morning had introduced a parameter error that effectively inverted the model's scoring logic. A corrective patch was issued at 7:45 PM. By 9:00 AM the following Monday, the module was operating normally.

The incident itself was contained relatively quickly. What followed required more careful navigation. The ISPM worked through the questions that the incident raised in sequence. How many loan decisions have been made or influenced by the anomalous recommendations during the

B. A. Salas, *AI Risk Management for Financial Institutions*,
https://doi.org/10.1007/979-8-8688-3353-3_15

two-hour window? The lending team identified eleven applications that had been reviewed during the affected period. Of those, three had received disposition decisions: two approvals and one denial, before the supervisor had halted the use of the recommendations.

Were those decisions affected by the anomalous outputs? The two approvals had been made for applicants whose profiles, when reviewed manually, supported the approval regardless of the AI recommendation. The denial had been made for an applicant whose profile was borderline. The loan officer confirmed that the AI recommendation score had influenced the decision. The denial would need to be reviewed.

Did the incident trigger GLBA notification obligations? The ISPM and compliance officer reviewed the incident against the Safeguards Rule notification criteria. The anomaly had not resulted in the unauthorized acquisition of member data. It had resulted in a potential adverse member impact from an incorrect AI output. The notification trigger was not met, but the member whose denial was under review needed to be contacted and the decision reconsidered.

Did the incident need to be reported to the board? The AI governance policy required board notification for any AI incident that resulted in member harm or regulatory notification. The potential member harm from the denial decision met the policy threshold. The board chair was briefed on the following Tuesday.

The ISPM documented the full incident timeline, the impact assessment, the member remediation actions, and the post-incident review findings. The incident report went to the Risk Committee at the next scheduled meeting. The post-incident review produced three process improvements: a monitoring alert for anomalous AI recommendation score distributions, a vendor requirement to notify the institution before any model configuration changes, and a lending policy update requiring supervisor review of all AI-influenced denials on borderline profiles.

The incident had been handled. The program was stronger for having handled it deliberately.

The Risk Problem

AI incidents differ from conventional technology incidents in ways that matter for response. A server outage has a clear start time, a clear resolution, and a clear scope of impact. An AI incident may involve behavior that is anomalous but not immediately obvious, impact that accumulates gradually before it is detected, member harm that is statistical rather than discrete, and regulatory obligations that depend on interpretive judgments about what "unauthorized acquisition" or "material harm" means in the context of AI system behavior.

The risk problem at the incident response layer is that most institutional incident response programs were designed for conventional technology failures, breaches, outages, and ransomware, and have not been extended to cover the distinct characteristics of AI incidents. An institution whose incident response plan does not include AI-specific scenarios, classification criteria, and response procedures will encounter an AI incident and improvise. Improvisation under regulatory scrutiny, with member harm on the table and GLBA notification timelines running, is a significantly more difficult situation than working from a prepared response framework.

The cross-functional nature of AI incident response compounds the improvisation risk. A conventional security incident is primarily owned by the security team. An AI incident implicates the security team, the risk manager, the compliance officer, the affected business unit, legal counsel, the vendor relationship manager, and potentially the board—simultaneously, with different questions and different decision authorities. Without a prepared response structure, coordinating that many stakeholders under time pressure produces delays, inconsistent decisions, and documentation gaps that are difficult to explain to an examiner after the fact.

Why It Matters to Credit Unions

For credit unions, AI incident response carries member stakes that extend beyond regulatory compliance. When an AI system causes a member to receive an incorrect lending decision, a false fraud flag that freezes their account, or a personalized communication based on data that should not have been used, the member's experience of that harm is direct and personal. The institution's response—how quickly it identifies the problem, how honestly it communicates with affected members, and how completely it remediates the harm—determines whether the incident damages the member relationship or strengthens it.

Credit unions that handle AI incidents with transparency and genuine member-first remediation are showing the cooperative values that distinguish the credit union model. Those who handle them defensively, minimizing disclosure, attributing responsibility to vendors, and delaying remediation, are failing the same test. AI incident response is one of the most direct expressions of institutional character in an AI governance program.

From a regulatory standpoint, the GLBA Safeguards Rule establishes notification obligations that apply to certain types of AI-related data incidents. The 2021 amendments require notification to the FTC within thirty days of discovering a notification event involving the unauthorized acquisition of unencrypted member data affecting five hundred or more members. AI incidents that result in unauthorized data exposure, member data processed through an unapproved tool, data retained by a vendor in violation of contract terms, or data exposed through a prompt injection attack may trigger this obligation. The institution needs a prepared assessment process that can evaluate notification requirements quickly, rather than working through the analysis from first principles under time pressure.

Governance and Risk Considerations

Effective AI incident response operates across five phases: detection and classification, containment, impact assessment, notification and escalation, and post-incident review. Each phase has AI-specific characteristics that distinguish it from conventional incident response.

Phase 1: Detection and Classification

AI incidents are detected through multiple channels: the monitoring program described in Chapter 11, staff reports of anomalous system behavior, member complaints, vendor notifications, and security alerts. Each channel produces a different initial signal quality; a monitoring alert for anomalous score distributions is more specific than a staff report that "something seems off" with the AI recommendations, and the initial response should calibrate to the signal quality available.

Classification determines the incident type, which drives the response track. AI incident types relevant to credit unions fall into four categories: performance anomalies (the system is producing outputs inconsistent with its documented behavior, as in the opening scenario); data incidents (member data has been improperly processed, retained, or exposed through an AI system); member harm incidents (an AI system's outputs have resulted in demonstrable harm to one or more members, including incorrect adverse decisions, false fraud flags, or discriminatory outcomes); and security incidents (an AI system has been targeted by adversarial attack, prompt injection, or other AI-specific threat vector).

Each incident type has a different primary response owner, different notification obligations, and different remediation paths. Classification should happen as early in the response as possible, ideally within the first hour of detection, so that the right response track is engaged before the incident evolves further.

Phase 2: Containment

Containment for AI incidents means stopping the harm from accumulating further. For performance anomalies, containment typically means suspending AI-influenced decisions in the affected area until the anomaly is resolved: exactly what the lending supervisor did in the opening scenario. For data incidents, containment means stopping the data flow that created the exposure and preserving evidence. For security incidents, containment follows the institution's standard incident response procedures extended to the AI system context.

The containment decision for AI incidents involves a judgment that conventional incidents rarely require a decision on whether to suspend the operational use of the AI system while the incident is investigated. That decision has a business impact: manual workflows are slower, staff are disrupted, and member-facing processes may be affected. The decision framework should be defined in advance rather than negotiated under pressure during an active incident. The governance policy should specify the conditions under which AI system suspension is required, recommended, or discretionary, so that the incident commander does not need to seek consensus on the question while the incident is running.

Phase 3: Impact Assessment

Impact assessment for AI incidents determines who was affected, how, and to what degree. For performance anomalies and member harm incidents, the assessment must identify the specific members whose interactions with the AI system occurred during the affected period, determine whether those interactions produced decisions or outcomes that were influenced by the anomalous behavior, and assess whether any of those outcomes caused demonstrable harm.

The data required for AI impact assessment, transaction logs, decision records, AI recommendation scores, and member interaction timestamps must be available and accessible within the response time frame. Institutions that discover during an incident that they cannot reconstruct the AI system's decision history for a specific time window are operating with a significant response capability gap. Logging requirements for AI systems should include the data needed for incident impact assessment, not just the data needed for normal operational monitoring.

For data incidents, the impact assessment must determine whether the GLBA notification threshold has been met. The assessment should be completed within the notification window, thirty days from discovery under the 2021 Safeguards Rule amendments and should produce a documented conclusion with supporting analysis rather than an informal judgment. That documentation is the institution's evidence that it applied the notification standard appropriately, regardless of whether notification was ultimately required.

Phase 4: Notification and Escalation

Notification and escalation for AI incidents run in three directions: internally to governance stakeholders, to affected members, and to regulators where required. Each notification track has different content requirements, different timing constraints, and different audience considerations.

Internal escalation should follow the protocol established in Chapter 13: the ISPM notifies the governance committee chair immediately for any incident meeting the defined escalation threshold; the full committee is engaged for member harm incidents, regulatory notification events, or incidents that cannot be resolved within a defined time frame; and the board is notified for incidents meeting the policy's board notification threshold. The escalation documentation should include the incident classification, the containment status, the preliminary impact assessment, and the notification obligations identified.

Member notification for AI-related harm should be prompt, honest, and specific. Members who received incorrect adverse decisions should be contacted directly, informed of the error, and offered remediation. Members whose data may have been improperly exposed should receive notification that is consistent with the institution's GLBA notification obligations and reflects the genuine member-first values of the cooperative model. The framing of member notification should not minimize the harm or attribute it entirely to a vendor: the institution is responsible for the AI systems it deploys, and that responsibility includes honest communication when those systems fail.

AI Incident Response: Classification and Response Track

Performance anomaly: ISPM + vendor • Suspend AI-influenced decisions • Vendor patch timeline

Data incident: ISPM + compliance + legal • Stop data flow • GLBA notification assessment within a 30-day window

Member harm: ISPM + compliance + business unit • Impact assessment • Member remediation • Board notification per policy threshold

Security incident: ISPM + security team • Standard IR procedures + AI-specific containment • Vendor notification • Threat intelligence sharing via FS-ISAC

Phase 5: Post-incident Review

The post-incident review is the governance activity that converts an incident from a failure into a program improvement. Every AI incident, regardless of severity, should produce a documented post-incident review within thirty days of resolution. The review should address four questions: What happened and why? What was the impact on members and the institution? What controls failed or were absent, and what would have prevented or limited the incident? What specific improvements to the AI governance program are required as a result?

The improvements identified in the post-incident review should enter the remediation tracking system as formal action items with owners, due dates, and governance committee oversight. They should not be treated as informal lessons learned that inform future practice without accountability. The incident report and the post-incident review, together with the remediation tracking record, constitute the institutional response record that demonstrates to examiners that the institution learns from AI incidents and improves its program in response.

Post-incident reviews should also inform the AI governance program's monitoring parameters, escalation thresholds, and incident response procedures. An incident that reveals a monitoring gap should produce an updated monitoring alert. An incident that revealed an ambiguous notification threshold should produce a policy clarification. An incident that revealed a response coordination failure should produce an updated incident response procedure. The program that improves continuously from experience is more defensible than the one that maintains static procedures regardless of what incidents reveal.

Tabletop Exercises for AI Incidents

The best time to discover that an AI incident response procedure does not work is during a tabletop exercise, not during an active incident. Tabletop exercises for AI-specific scenarios should be conducted at least annually and should test the full response cycle: detection, classification, containment, impact assessment, notification, and post-incident review. The exercise does not need to be elaborate; a two-hour facilitated discussion using a realistic scenario suffices to surface gaps in the response procedure and build the cross-functional familiarity that makes coordinated incident response possible.

Scenarios for AI tabletop exercises should be drawn from the incident types most likely in the institution's specific AI environment. An institution with a vendor fraud detection model should run an adversarial probing scenario. An institution with a member-facing chatbot should run a prompt injection scenario. An institution with an AI-assisted lending system should run a performance anomaly scenario similar to the opening scenario in this chapter. The scenario should be realistic enough to surface genuine response challenges rather than abstract enough to produce only theoretical discussion. A well-structured AI tabletop invites the full cross-functional response team: the ISPM, the risk manager, the compliance officer, a representative from the affected business unit, and the vendor relationship manager if a vendor AI system is involved. A designated facilitator presents the scenario in stages—initial detection signal, first containment decision, impact assessment question, notification trigger—pausing after each stage so participants work through their actual response rather than a theoretical one. The gaps that surface—the question no one can answer, the notification threshold no one is certain about, the vendor contact information no one has current—are the exercise's output. Each gap becomes a formal remediation item. The post-exercise debrief, conducted immediately after while the gaps are fresh, is where the governance value concentrates. The next year's tabletop begins where the last one ended.

Implementation Steps

1. Add AI incident classification criteria and response tracks to the institution's existing incident response plan. Define the four AI incident types: performance anomaly, data incident, member harm, and security

incident, and specify the primary response owner, containment approach, notification obligations, and escalation path for each. The addition does not require rewriting the existing plan; it requires an AI-specific annex that integrates with the existing structure.

2. Define the AI system suspension decision framework in the incident response plan. Specify the conditions under which AI system use must be suspended immediately, recommended for suspension pending assessment, or may continue with enhanced manual oversight. The framework should be specific enough to guide the incident commander's decisions without requiring consensus from multiple stakeholders under time pressure.

3. Verify that logging and data retention for each AI system support impact assessment requirements. Confirm that the data needed to reconstruct the AI system's decision history for a defined look-back period, recommendation scores, input parameters, decision timestamps, and member identifiers, is being captured and retained. Document any gaps and add them to the remediation plan as high-priority items, given their incident response dependency.

4. Develop a GLBA notification assessment checklist specific to AI data incidents. The checklist should walk through the notification criteria in the 2021 Safeguards Rule amendments, apply them to

AI-specific data incident scenarios, and produce a documented yes/no notification conclusion with supporting analysis. The checklist should be reviewed by the compliance officer and legal counsel before it is needed in an incident rather than during one.

5. Conduct an AI incident tabletop exercise within the next twelve months. Select a scenario appropriate to the institution's highest-risk AI system, invite the full cross-functional response team, and run the full response cycle. Document gaps identified and enter them into the remediation tracking system. Schedule the next tabletop as a standing annual governance calendar item.

Important Points

- AI incidents differ from conventional technology incidents in detection characteristics, impact assessment complexity, cross-functional coordination requirements, and regulatory notification analysis. Conventional incident response plans must be explicitly extended to cover AI-specific scenarios.
- The four AI incident types—performance anomaly, data incident, member harm, and security incident—each have distinct response owners, notification obligations, and remediation paths. Classification at the outset of an incident determines which response track is engaged.

- The AI system suspension decision is a judgment that must be defined in advance. Negotiating under time pressure during an active incident produces delays, inconsistent decisions, and governance gaps.
- Post-incident reviews should produce formal program improvements with governance committee oversight, not informal lessons learned. The institutional response record, incident report, post-incident review, and remediation tracking are the examination of evidence that the institution learns and improves.
- Tabletop exercises are the most efficient investment in AI incident response capabilities. Two hours of facilitated scenario discussion produced more response readiness than any amount of procedure documentation that has not been tested.

Questions for Leadership

1. Does our incident response plan include AI-specific incident classification criteria, response tracks, and escalation procedures, or does it address only conventional technology incident types?
2. Is the AI system suspension decision framework defined in advance with specific criteria, or would a suspension decision during an active incident require real-time consensus from multiple stakeholders?

3. Do our AI systems retain the logging and decision history data needed to conduct an impact assessment for a two-week look-back period, and has that capability been verified rather than assumed?

4. Has the compliance officer reviewed and approved a GLBA notification assessment checklist specific to AI data incidents, and is that checklist accessible to the incident response team?

5. When was our most recent AI incident tabletop exercise? What scenarios were tested, and what improvements did it produce? Is the next tabletop on the governance calendar?

Further Reading

- GLBA Safeguards Rule, 16 CFR Part 314, Section 314.15: Notification Requirements for Data Breaches—FTC.
- NIST AI RMF, MANAGE Function: AI Incident Response and Recovery—NIST.
- NCUA Letter 21-CU-04: Ransomware and Cyber Incident Notification Requirements—NCUA.
- FFIEC IT Examination Handbook, Business Continuity Booklet: Incident Response and Recovery—FFIEC.
- NIST SP 800-61 Rev. 3: Computer Security Incident Handling Guide—NIST.

PART V

Strategic Oversight and the Future

Chapters 16–18 address the view from the top: board engagement with AI risk, responsible AI as a cooperative value, and the regulatory and technological trends that will define AI governance in the years ahead.

CHAPTER 16

Board Oversight of AI Risk

Opening Scenario

The ISPM had fifteen minutes on the board agenda. He had done board presentations before: cybersecurity program updates, incident briefings, compliance status reviews, and he understood the audience. Volunteer directors with careers in lending, accounting, community development, and small business. Thoughtful, engaged, and genuinely invested in the credit union's success. Not technical. Not expected to be.

His first instinct had been to build a slide deck that walked through the AI governance program in sequence: the inventory, the risk assessments, the committee structure, and the monitoring program. He had drafted twelve slides before he stopped and asked himself a different question: what does the board actually need to know to exercise meaningful oversight of AI risk at this institution?

The answer was not a program tour. The board needed to know three things. First, what AI is doing in the institution right now—not in technical terms, but in terms of which decisions affecting members are being influenced or made by AI systems. Second, what the significant risks are and what the institution is doing about them—expressed in terms of potential member impact and regulatory exposure, not in terms of governance framework layers. Third, what the board is being asked to

B. A. Salas, *AI Risk Management for Financial Institutions*,
https://doi.org/10.1007/979-8-8688-3353-3_16

do—whether they are being asked to approve something, provide direction on something, or simply be informed of something so that their oversight is documented.

He rebuilt the deck around those three questions. Five slides. Twelve minutes of presentation and three minutes of questions. The board chair asked two questions that were substantive, specific, and reflected a genuine engagement with the content. The minutes documented that the board had received an AI governance briefing, reviewed the institution's AI risk posture, and noted the program's forward agenda.

After the meeting, the board chair stopped the ISPM in the hallway. "That was the first presentation about a technology risk topic where I actually understood what you were telling us and what you needed from us," she says. "Do that every year."

The Risk Problem

The risk problem at the board oversight layer of the AI Governance Pyramid is the gap between formal oversight and substantive oversight. Formal oversight means that the board receives AI governance briefings, that those briefings appear in the meeting minutes, and that the institution can point to documentation of board engagement when an examiner asks. Substantive oversight means that board members actually understand what they are being told, ask questions that reflect genuine engagement, and make or ratify governance decisions from an informed position.

The gap between formal and substantive oversight is primarily a communication problem. Most AI governance briefings are designed by practitioners who understand the subject deeply and are presented to audiences who do not. The practitioner's instinct is to convey the depth of their knowledge: to show program sophistication through comprehensive coverage of frameworks, processes, and metrics. The board's need is for distilled clarity: what matters, why it matters, and what they are expected to do about it.

When the gap is wide, when board members are receiving technically dense briefings that they cannot meaningfully engage with, two failure modes emerge. The first is passive approval: the board notes the briefing and moves on without substantive engagement, producing a documentation record of oversight without the reality of it. The second is governance fatigue: board members who consistently receive presentations they cannot engage with become disengaged from the governance process, reducing the quality of oversight not just for AI but for other risk topics that share the same board agenda.

Why It Matters to Credit Unions

Credit union boards are composed of volunteer directors who bring diverse professional backgrounds and genuine community commitment to their governance roles. They are not technology professionals, and the governance model does not require them to be. What it requires is that they receive information about AI risk in a form that allows them to exercise the judgment they were elected to provide: assessing whether management's approach to a significant risk is sound, asking the questions that a reasonable fiduciary would ask, and making or approving decisions that reflect the institution's values and risk appetite.

NCUA examiners assess board oversight of AI governance by reviewing board meeting minutes for evidence of substantive engagement. Minutes that record only that a briefing was received, with no sign of board questions, discussion, or decisions, suggest formal rather than substantive oversight. Minutes that record specific questions the board asked, the responses they received, and the decisions or directions that resulted suggest genuine engagement. The quality of board engagement documented in the minutes is a direct indicator of the quality of oversight the examiner will assess.

For the ISPM, meaningful board engagement with AI governance is also a resource and authority outcome. A board that understands AI risk, has engaged with the program's priorities, and has formally approved the governance framework is a board that will support the resource requests and policy decisions the program requires. That is not a compliance outcome. Board understanding is a program enabler.

Governance and Risk Considerations

Effective board oversight of AI risk requires three capabilities: a briefing framework that produces substantive engagement rather than passive reception, a set of defined board-level decision authorities that connect governance activities to the board's formal role, and a documentation practice that creates an examination-defensible record of board oversight over time.

The Board AI Briefing Framework

The annual board AI governance briefing should be structured around three questions that board members can meaningfully engage with: What is AI doing in our institution? What are the significant risks, and what is management doing about them? What does the board need to decide or affirm?

What is AI doing in our institution should be answered in member-impact language, not technical language. Rather than describing the AI systems in the inventory by their technical function, describe what they do for or to members: the system that recommends whether to approve a member's loan application, the system that flags unusual transactions on a member's account, the system that routes member service inquiries to the right support channel. This framing makes the scope of AI activity legible to board members and connects it to the member relationship, which is the board's primary fiduciary focus.

What are the significant risks? It should present the two or three highest-residual-risk items from the current AI risk assessment cycle, described in terms of potential member impact and regulatory exposure. The board does not need to understand the technical mechanisms of model opacity or adversarial attacks. They need to understand that there is a system making consequential member decisions that the institution cannot fully explain, which creates both member harm risk and regulatory exposure, and that management is pursuing specific remediation actions with a defined timeline. Severity, impact, and management response, in that order, is the framework that produces board engagement.

What does the board need to decide or affirm should be explicit rather than implicit. If the briefing is informational, say so. If the board is being asked to formally adopt the AI governance framework, approve a significant AI deployment, or affirm the institution's AI risk appetite statement, that request should be the final agenda item with a clear motion and vote. Boards that know what is expected of them engage more substantively than boards that are uncertain whether they are being asked to act or merely to listen.

Board-Level Decision Authorities

The AI governance framework should define which decisions require board-level authority versus executive or committee authority. Board-level decisions for AI governance typically include formal adoption of the AI governance policy and its periodic updates; approval of the institution's AI risk appetite statement; notification of and formal acknowledgment of significant AI incidents meeting the policy's board notification threshold; and any AI deployment that represents a strategic capability shift for the institution—Level 4 autonomous systems that would materially change how consequential member decisions are made.

Defining board-level decision authorities in the governance policy serves two purposes. It ensures that the board's formal governance role is exercised for decisions that genuinely warrant it, rather than being bypassed by operational convenience. And it protects the board from being placed in a position of retroactively ratifying decisions that should have come to them in advance—a situation that creates both governance quality problems and examination documentation challenges. Each board-level AI governance decision should appear in the meeting minutes as a formal action item: a motion made, a vote recorded, and the outcome documented. This creates an examination-defensible record that authorization preceded the action rather than followed it. A board that adopted the AI governance policy in January, approved the risk appetite statement in April, and received formal notification of a significant incident in September has a documented oversight record. A board that received informational briefings on all three does not.

Structuring the AI Risk Appetite Statement

The AI risk appetite statement is the board's most direct expression of its AI governance expectations. It does not need to be technically detailed; it needs to be specific enough to guide management decisions and clear enough that board members can assess whether the institution's AI activities are consistent with what was approved.

A credit union AI risk appetite statement should address four dimensions. Member impact appetite: the institution will not deploy autonomous AI systems that make final decisions affecting member credit or account access without a human review process. Data protection appetite: the institution will not permit member financial data to be used by AI systems for purposes other than those for which it was collected without explicit governance approval and, where required, member consent. Transparency appetite: the institution will only deploy AI systems in lending and member-facing decision contexts where it can provide a meaningful explanation of adverse decisions to affected members. Regulatory exposure appetite: the institution will maintain a documented AI governance program that meets or exceeds NCUA and FFIEC examination expectations for an institution of its size and AI complexity.

The risk appetite statement does not need to be a lengthy document. Four logical statements of what the institution will and will not do with AI, approved by the board and referenced in the governance policy, provide the directional authority that management needs and the accountability framework that oversight requires.

The Five-Slide Board AI Briefing Structure

Slide 1: What AI is doing in our institution—member-impact descriptions of active AI systems

Slide 2: Our AI risk posture—classification summary, high/critical items, trend vs. prior year

Slide 3: Significant risks and management response—top 2–3 risks, impact language, remediation status

Slide 4: Program health—governance committee activity, exam readiness, forward agenda

Slide 5: What we need from the board—explicit decision items or a formal acknowledgment request

Target: 12–15 minutes presentation, 5–10 minutes questions, documented in minutes

---

Documentation for Examination Readiness

The board oversight record for AI governance should be maintained as a discrete documentation set that can be produced quickly in response to an examiner's request. The set should include the board meeting minutes from each AI governance briefing, the briefing materials presented, any formal resolutions or votes related to AI governance decisions, the AI risk appetite statement with its adoption date and any subsequent amendments, and the board's notification and acknowledgment records for any significant AI incidents.

Minutes quality matters as much as minutes completeness. Minutes that record only that an AI briefing was received are weaker evidence of substantive oversight than minutes that record the specific questions board members asked, the responses management provided, any concerns the board expressed, and the formal actions taken. The ISPM can support minutes quality by providing the board secretary with a suggested minutes framework after each AI briefing: a brief description of what was presented and what the board discussed that the secretary can incorporate into the formal record.

Consistent annual briefings, documented with substantive engagement evidence, build a multi-year oversight record that is meaningfully more defensible than a single comprehensive briefing after years of inactivity. Examiners reviewing the three-year governance record of an institution that briefed its board annually, documented genuine board questions and responses, and formally adopted governance policy updates will draw very different conclusions than examiners reviewing the record of an institution that produced one briefing deck in response to examination notice.

Implementation Steps

1. Rebuild the board AI briefing around the three-question framework and the five-slide structure. If a board briefing deck already exists, assess it against the structure: Does it lead with member-impact descriptions of AI activity? Does it present

significant risks in impact language rather than technical terms? Does it end with an explicit request for board action or acknowledgment? Revise as needed before the next scheduled briefing.

2. Draft the AI risk appetite statement for board adoption. Use the four-dimension framework—member impact, data protection, transparency, and regulatory exposure—as the organizing structure. Draft in plain language that board members can read, understand, and meaningfully ratify. Submit to the AI Governance Committee for review before bringing it to the board and confirm legal counsel has reviewed the draft.

3. Define board-level decision authorities in the AI governance policy. Add a section that specifies which AI governance decisions require board approval versus executive or committee authority. Ensure the board notification threshold for AI incidents is specific, documented in the policy, and referenced in the incident response plan.

4. Establish a practice of providing the board secretary with a suggested minutes framework after each AI briefing. The framework should describe what was presented, note any significant discussion points or board questions, and identify any formal actions taken. This investment of fifteen minutes after each meeting significantly improves the quality of the oversight record over time.

5. Schedule the annual board AI governance briefing as a standing item on the board's governance calendar. If it is not on the calendar, it will compete with other priorities and be deferred. The standing calendar item signals that AI governance oversight is an expected, recurring board responsibility rather than an ad hoc update when the ISPM requests time.

Important Points

- The gap between formal and substantive board oversight is primarily a communication problem. Briefings designed for practitioners produce passive reception from non-technical boards. Briefings designed for the audience produce genuine engagement.
- The three-question briefing framework: What is AI doing in our institution? What are the significant risks, and what is management doing? What does the board need to decide? This produces substantive engagement that distinguishes oversight from documentation.
- The AI risk appetite statement is the board's most direct expression of AI governance expectations. Four logical statements covering member impact, data protection, transparency, and regulatory exposure provide directional authority without requiring technical depth.
- Board-level decision authorities should be defined in the governance policy so that the board's formal

governance role is exercised for decisions that genuinely warrant it, not bypassed by operational convenience or retroactively ratified after the fact.

- Minutes quality is as important as the briefing frequency. A multi-year record of substantive engagement documented in board minutes is the most examination-defensible evidence of meaningful board oversight of AI risk. Examination readiness, however, is only one measure of program quality. The other—whether the institution's AI governance reflects the values it owes its members—is addressed in Chapter 17.

Questions for Leadership

1. Does our board AI brief present AI activity in member-impact terms, significant risks in impact language, and end with an explicit request for board action or acknowledgment?
2. Has the board formally adopted an AI risk appetite statement that addresses member impact, data protection, transparency, and regulatory exposure in plain, board-accessible language?
3. Are the board-level AI governance decision authorities defined in the governance policy, and have all decisions requiring board approval been brought to the board rather than handled at the executive or committee level?

4. Do board meeting minutes from AI governance briefings reflect substantive engagement, specific questions, management responses, board concerns, and formal actions, or do they record only that a briefing was received?
5. Is the annual board AI governance briefing scheduled as a standing item in the board's governance calendar for the coming year?

Further Reading

- NCUA Supervisory Letter: Board of Directors Responsibilities and Governance Expectations—NCUA.
- FFIEC IT Examination Handbook, Management Booklet: Board and Senior Management Responsibilities—FFIEC.
- NIST AI RMF, GOVERN Function: Senior Leadership and Board Engagement in AI Risk—NIST.
- COSO ERM Framework: Board Oversight and Governance Culture—Committee of Sponsoring Organizations.
- National Association of Corporate Directors: AI Governance Principles for Board Directors—NACD.

CHAPTER 17

Responsible AI and Member Trust

Opening Scenario

The letter arrived in the mail on a Wednesday. Not an email—a handwritten letter from a member who had been with the credit union for thirty-one years. She had recently been declined for a home equity loan. The decline letter cited "scoring criteria" without further explanation. She had called member services twice and been told the decision was final. She was writing to the ISPM because someone at the branch had mentioned that a computer system was involved in loan decisions, and she thought he might be able to help her understand.

She was not angry in the letter. She was confused. She had been a member since she was twenty-four years old. She had held a checking account, a savings account, a vehicle loan, and a credit card with the credit union across three decades. She had never missed a payment. Her income had been stable for years. She did not understand what scoring criteria could have produced a denial that no human being had explained to her in terms she could comprehend.

The ISPM forwarded the letter to the lending department and the compliance officer with a single question: Can we explain this decision to this member in plain language? The lending team pulled the application. The AI-assisted underwriting tool had flagged a debt-to-income ratio that

B. A. Salas, *AI Risk Management for Financial Institutions*,
https://doi.org/10.1007/979-8-8688-3353-3_17

exceeded the model's recommendation threshold by a small margin. The loan officer followed the recommendation without further review. The adverse action notice had been generated automatically with standard regulatory language that technically satisfied ECOA requirements but communicated almost nothing meaningful to the member.

The compliance officer confirmed that the notice met the minimum legal standard. The ISPM sat with that answer for a moment before responding. Meeting the minimum legal standard and honoring a thirty-one-year member relationship were not the same thing. An AI system had recommended a denial. A loan officer had accepted that recommendation without a meaningful review of the member's full relationship history. The notice had explained nothing. Three decades of demonstrated trustworthiness had been evaluated by a model that knew nothing about the member as a person and communicated its conclusion through a form letter.

He drafted a response to the member's letter personally. He explained what had happened in plain language. He told her that her application had been reviewed by an AI system and that the system's recommendation had not fully accounted for her full relationship with the credit union. He told her that the application was being reconsidered by a senior loan officer who would review her complete member history. And he told her that the credit union was improving its processes to ensure that AI-assisted decisions were reviewed more thoughtfully before they were communicated to members.

The reconsideration produced an approval. The process improvement produced a policy requiring senior loan officer review of any AI-influenced denial for members with five or more years of continuous membership and no delinquency history.

The letter had arrived as a complaint. It left as the most useful governance input the AI program had received all year.

The Risk Problem

The risk addressed in this chapter is different in character from the risks covered in the preceding sixteen chapters. It is not a compliance risk, a security risk, or an operational risk in the conventional sense. It is an integrity risk—the risk that the institution's use of AI is inconsistent with the values that define what a credit union is supposed to be.

The cooperative model was built on the premise that distinguishes credit unions from every other type of financial institution: the institution exists to serve its members, not to profit from them. Members are owners. Their financial well-being is the institution's primary purpose. Every governance decision the institution makes, including decisions about AI, is ultimately accountable to that premise.

AI systems, applied without care, can systematically violate that premise in ways that are invisible precisely because they operate at scale. A loan officer who denies a thirty-one-year member without meaningful review is making a judgment that leadership can observe and correct. An AI system that generates the same outcome for thousands of similar members creates a systematic pattern of outcomes that no individual decision-maker reviews and no individual member complaint fully reveals. The scale of AI's reach is what makes the responsible AI question not just an ethical consideration but a governance imperative.

Why It Matters to Credit Unions

The credit union movement has a specific and hard-won identity in the American financial landscape. Credit unions exist in communities that have been underserved by conventional banking. They were often found specifically to provide access to financial services for people whom banks declined to serve. Their history is one of financial inclusion, community investment, and genuine member-first service.

AI systems deployed without responsible governance can systematically undermine that history. A fraud detection model trained on behavioral data from a different population may generate disproportionate false positives for the credit union's lower-income or minority members, exactly the members the institution was founded to serve. A lending model that weighs certain credit bureau data patterns heavily may reproduce and amplify historical credit access inequities that the credit union was explicitly created to counteract. A collections AI that optimizes outreach timing for maximum payment recovery may do so in ways that are technically effective, but that treat financially stressed members as optimization targets rather than as people the institution has a relationship with.

None of these outcomes are inevitable. They are the predictable result of deploying AI without the governance structures that evaluate AI outputs against the institution's values, not just against its technical performance metrics. Responsible AI governance asks a question that purely technical AI governance does not: are the outcomes this system produces consistent with who we are and what we are here to do?

Governance and Risk Considerations

Responsible AI governance at a credit union operates across four dimensions: fairness and equity in AI outcomes, transparency with members about AI use, human dignity in AI-assisted interactions, and accountability when AI produces harm. Each dimension connects directly to the cooperative values that define the institution's identity.

Fairness and Equity in AI Outcomes

Fairness in AI outcomes means that AI systems do not produce systematically different results for members based on characteristics that should be irrelevant to the decision being made, and particularly that they do not produce outcomes that disadvantage members based on protected class characteristics or proxies for those characteristics. For credit unions, this is not only a legal obligation under ECOA and the Fair Housing Act. It is a founding value.

Operationalizing fairness requires more than compliance with adverse action notice requirements. It requires the outcome analysis process described in Chapters 5 and 11: periodic review of AI-assisted decision patterns across demographic segments to identify disparities that statistical analysis can surface even when individual decisions appear reasonable. A credit union that conducts quarterly outcome analysis for its AI lending model and finds no statistically significant disparity has evidence of fairness. One that has never conducted the analysis cannot make that claim, regardless of its intentions.

Fairness also requires that the human review mechanisms around AI systems are designed to catch and correct unfair outcomes before they accumulate into patterns. The policy improvement described in the opening scenario, requiring senior loan officer review for AI-influenced denials of long-term members with clean payment histories, is a proportionate, values-driven control that supplements the AI system's technical performance with human judgment calibrated to the member relationship.

Transparency with Members

Transparency means members can understand, in plain language, how AI systems affect decisions about their accounts and services. This goes beyond the legal minimum of adverse action notices that satisfy ECOA by citing generic scoring criteria. It means that when a member asks why a decision was made, the institution can provide an honest, comprehensible answer that respects the member's intelligence and their right to understand decisions that affect their financial life.

Transparency also means that the institution is honest with members about the role AI plays in its operations. This does not require proactive disclosure of every AI capability in every member interaction. It requires that when a member asks whether AI was involved in a decision; they receive an honest answer. And it requires that the institution's communications about AI, in member newsletters, annual reports, or website disclosures, are accurate and not designed to minimize or obscure the degree to which AI influences member-facing decisions.

The transparency standard that responsible AI governance sets is the standard that any member should be able to apply: if my credit union were fully transparent with me about how AI is used in decisions about my account, would I find that use consistent with the relationship I thought I had with this institution? That question, asked regularly by the governance program, is a more demanding standard than regulatory minimum compliance and a more appropriate one for a cooperative institution.

Human Dignity in AI-Assisted Interactions

Human dignity in AI-assisted interactions means that AI systems are designed and deployed in ways that treat members as people with complex financial lives, histories, and circumstances rather than as data points to be optimized. This dimension is the hardest to operationalize; it resists reduction to a checklist or a metric, but it is the most directly connected to the member experience of the institution's values.

The opening scenario illustrates the human dignity dimension in concrete terms. The AI system had processed the member's application accurately against its model parameters. The adverse action notice had met the legal standard. And yet the outcome, a form letter declining a thirty-one-year-old member without explanation or human acknowledgment of her history, failed the human dignity test. The system had treated her as a data input rather than as a person with a relationship.

Governance mechanisms that protect human dignity include: requiring human review for AI-assisted adverse decisions on members with significant relationship history; designing adverse action communications that go beyond the legal minimum to provide genuinely useful explanations; building escalation pathways that allow members to request human review of AI-influenced decisions; and establishing member feedback mechanisms that surface dignity failures before they accumulate into patterns that damage the member relationship at scale.

Accountability When AI Produces Harm

Accountability means that when AI systems produce outcomes that harm members, make incorrect adverse decisions, discriminatory patterns, privacy violations, or dignity failures, the institution acknowledges the harm, remediates it, and changes the practice that produced it. Accountability is what distinguishes an institution that treats AI governance as a genuine commitment from one that treats it as a compliance exercise.

The accountability standard for credit unions should be higher than the legal minimum precisely because the cooperative model promises more than minimum compliance. A credit union that remediates an AI-related member harm only when legally compelled to is operating below the standard its own values set. One that proactively identifies potential harms through monitoring, reaches out to affected members before they complain, and changes its practices to prevent recurrence is demonstrating the member-first orientation that the cooperative model requires.

Accountability also has an internal dimension. When an AI governance failure occurs, when a system was deployed without adequate review, when a monitoring gap allowed harm to accumulate, when a vendor's model produced discriminatory outcomes, the institution had not assessed, the post-incident review should produce honest internal accountability, not defensive attribution. The institution that learns from its AI governance failures and improves continuously is building the program that the cooperative model deserves.

Responsible AI: The Four Governance Questions

Fairness: Do this system's outcomes treat all members equitably, and do we have evidence from outcome analysis to support that conclusion?

Transparency: Can we explain this system's role in member decisions in plain language, honestly and completely, to any member who asks?

Human dignity: Does this system treat members as people with complex financial lives and relationships, or as data inputs to be processed?

Accountability: When this system produces harm, do we acknowledge it, remediate it, and change the practice that produced it—before being required to?

Responsible AI As a Competitive Distinction

Responsible AI governance is not only a values obligation; it is a strategic asset. As AI becomes more prevalent in financial services, the institutions that can demonstrate to members that their AI use is governed by the same member-first values that define their broader operations will have a meaningful distinction from financial institutions that deploy AI primarily for operational efficiency without equivalent member-protection governance.

Credit unions that publish a clear, plain-language statement of their AI governance commitments, what they will and will not do with AI, how they protect member data, how they ensure fair treatment, how members can request human review, are offering something that most financial institutions cannot credibly offer: an AI governance model built around the people the institution serves rather than the operational outcomes the institution wants to achieve. That distinction is worth communicating. It is one of the most authentic expressions of the credit union difference in the AI era.

Implementation Steps

1. Conduct a responsible AI audit of each Level 3 and Level 4 AI system against the four dimensions: fairness (with outcome analysis evidence), transparency (with member communication review), human dignity (with human review mechanism assessment), and accountability (with incident response and remediation record review). Document the findings and present them to the governance committee as a responsible AI program health assessment.
2. Review adverse action notice practices for all AI-assisted lending and account decisions. Assess whether current notices provide genuinely useful explanations or satisfy only the legal minimum. Develop enhanced notice language that explains the role of AI in plain terms and provides members with a clear pathway to request human review. Submit the enhanced language to legal and compliance review before implementation.

3. Establish a member escalation pathway for AI-influenced decisions. Define the process by which any member can request that an AI-assisted decision be reviewed by a human decision-maker with full knowledge of the member's relationship history. Document the pathway in member-facing communications and train member services staff to explain it clearly.

4. Draft a member-facing responsible AI statement for the credit union's website or member communications. The statement should describe, in plain language, how AI is used in member-facing decisions, what governance commitments the institution has made to protect member interests, and how members can exercise their rights with respect to AI-assisted decisions. Submit to marketing, compliance, and legal for review before publication.

5. Incorporate the four responsible AI governance questions into the annual risk assessment cycle for Level 3 and Level 4 systems. The assessment record for each system should include an explicit evaluation against each dimension, not just the technical risk assessment criteria established in Chapter 5. This embeds responsible AI as a standing governance requirement rather than a periodic values exercise.

Important Points

- Responsible AI governance addresses an integrity risk that conventional risk frameworks do not capture: the risk that AI deployment is inconsistent with the cooperative values that define what a credit union is supposed to be.
- The four dimensions of responsible AI governance—fairness, transparency, human dignity, and accountability—each connect directly to the member-first orientation of the cooperative model, and each requires specific governance mechanisms to operationalize.
- Fairness requires outcome analysis evidence, not just the absence of discriminatory intent. A credit union that has never conducted demographic outcome analysis for its AI lending decisions cannot credibly claim to have assessed fairness.
- The transparency standard appropriate for a cooperative institution goes beyond legal minimum adverse action notice compliance. Members deserve to understand, in plain language, how AI affects decisions about their financial lives.
- Responsible AI is both a values obligation and a strategic distinction. Credit unions that govern AI with a genuine member-first commitment have a differentiator that most financial institutions cannot credibly claim.

Questions for Leadership

1. Have we conducted demographic outcome analysis for each AI system that influences member credit or account decisions, and do we have documented evidence that those systems are producing fair outcomes across the member population?
2. Do our adverse action notices for AI-assisted decisions provide genuinely useful explanations in plain language, or do they satisfy only the legal minimum in ways that leave members without a meaningful understanding of the decision?
3. Is there a defined pathway for members to request human review of AI-assisted decisions, and is that pathway communicated clearly in member-facing materials and by member services staff?
4. Does our institution have a published, plain-language statement of its AI governance commitments that members can read and hold us accountable too?
5. When we evaluate AI systems in the annual risk assessment cycle, do we explicitly assess them against responsible AI dimensions—fairness, transparency, human dignity, and accountability—as well as technical risk criteria?

Further Reading

- CFPB Circular 2022-03: Adverse Action Notification Requirements and Explainability—Consumer Financial Protection Bureau.
- NIST AI RMF, GOVERN Function: Trustworthy AI Characteristics and Responsible Deployment—NIST.
- NCUA Fair Lending Examination Procedures: Disparate Impact and Algorithmic Decision-Making—NCUA.
- Credit Union National Association: Principles for Member-Centered AI Use in Credit Unions—CUNA.
- Partnership on AI: Responsible AI Practices for Financial Services—Partnership on AI.

CHAPTER 18

The Future of AI Governance in Financial Services

Chapter 18 departs from the standard chapter structure. This chapter addresses the forward horizon of AI governance and closes with a reflection on the journey this book has described. The Implementation Steps, Important Points, Questions for Leadership, and Further Reading sections present in Chapters 1–17 are not included here; the Closing Reflection that ends this chapter serves in their place.

Opening Scenario

Two years had passed since the ISPM had first presented a half-finished AI inventory to the Risk Committee and watched the room go quiet. The program that had grown from that moment bore almost no resemblance to the ad hoc collection of activities it had started as. There was a current, maintained inventory. There were risk assessments for every system in it. There was a functioning governance committee with documented meeting records and a board that received annual briefings it could genuinely

B. A. Salas, *AI Risk Management for Financial Institutions*,
https://doi.org/10.1007/979-8-8688-3353-3_18

engage with. There were vendor contracts with AI-specific provisions, a monitoring program that caught anomalies before they became incidents, and an acceptable use policy that staff had actually read.

At the most recent NCUA examination, the examiner had spent ninety minutes reviewing the AI governance program. She had asked to see the inventory, the risk assessments, two recent committee meeting minutes, the board briefing from the prior year, and the monitoring report for the current quarter. She had reviewed each document in sequence. At the end of the review, she had noted one item for follow-up, a contract renewal that was ninety days overdue for an AI-specific addendum and had otherwise described the program as well-structured and appropriately scaled for the institution's size and AI risk profile.

The ISPM had written that outcome up in a brief internal memo that he shared with the CEO and the board chair. He noted that the program had taken approximately eighteen months of consistent work to build and that it was now in a maintenance and improvement posture rather than a construction posture. He estimated that the ongoing governance activities required approximately four to six hours per week of his time, with peaks around quarterly committee meetings and the annual board briefing. The program was sustainable.

He had also noted something in the memo that was harder to quantify but felt important: the credit union's relationship with AI had changed. Two years ago, AI had been something that arrived in the environment without anyone fully understanding where it came from or what it was doing. Now it was something the institution understood, managed, and made deliberate decisions about. Business unit leaders brought AI tool proposals to the ISPM before adopting them rather than after. The governance committee reviewed deployment decisions before they were made rather than incidents after they had occurred. The board asked questions about AI at each annual briefing that were more specific and more informed than the questions from the year before.

The program had not only reduced the risk. It had changed the institution's relationship with technology, which was going to become more significant, not less, in the years ahead. That change, from passive recipient to informed steward, was the outcome the ISPM had been working toward from the beginning.

The Risk Problem

The final risk problem this book addresses is not a current risk; it is a future risk. The institutions that build proportionate, defensible AI governance programs today are preparing for an environment that will be significantly more demanding than the one they currently operate in. The regulatory expectations that currently express themselves as examiner questions and matters requiring attention will harden into formal guidance, examination modules, and potentially rule-making over the next several years. The AI capabilities that currently arrive as vendor feature additions will become more autonomous, more consequential, and more deeply embedded in institutional operations. The members who currently ask occasional questions about AI will develop more sophisticated expectations about transparency, fairness, and control.

Institutions that have not built governance programs by the time this environment arrives will face a construction effort under examination pressure rather than in advance of it. The difference between building a governance program deliberately, over eighteen months, with the institutional will and resources to do it well and building one reactively in response to an examination finding is not just a difference in timeline. It is a difference in quality, sustainability, and the institutional culture within which the program operates.

The risk of waiting is not that the regulatory environment will be unkind to unprepared institutions—though it may be. The risk is that the institutions that wait will miss the window in which building a governance program is primarily a program management challenge and enter a window in which it is simultaneously a program management challenge and an examination remediation exercise. The latter is harder, more expensive, and produces programs that are built to satisfy an examiner rather than to genuinely govern the institution's AI activities.

Why It Matters to Credit Unions

Credit unions that build strong AI governance programs today are positioning themselves as the standard-setters for responsible AI adoption in the cooperative financial services sector. The credit union movement has historically led to member-first values, community investment, and financial inclusion—areas where the cooperative model's values produce genuinely different institutional behavior than the profit motive produces elsewhere. AI governance is the next arena in which those values can produce leadership rather than followership.

The practical benefit of early governance investment is resilience. Institutions with mature AI governance programs are better positioned to evaluate and adopt new AI capabilities as they emerge because the governance infrastructure needed to assess and manage those capabilities already exists. They are better positioned to respond to regulatory developments because their programs are built on the sound foundations that those developments will formalize. And they are better positioned to manage AI incidents when they occur, because the response capabilities have been built and tested in advance rather than improvised under pressure.

For the credit union movement as a whole, broad adoption of responsible AI governance practices creates collective resilience. When credit unions across the sector govern AI with the same member-first values that define their other operations, the sector builds a track record that shapes regulatory expectations, informs industry guidance, and demonstrates that small financial institutions can govern emerging technology as thoughtfully as any large enterprise—often more thoughtfully, because the member relationship that governs their decisions is immediate and personal rather than abstract and statistical.

Governance and Risk Considerations

Five trends that institutions should monitor shape the forward governance landscape for AI in financial services, plan for, and sometimes actively contribute to shaping.

Trend 1: Regulatory Formalization

Principle-based expectations characterize the current regulatory environment for AI in financial services, expressed through existing frameworks, SR 11-7, the FFIEC handbook, GLBA, and consumer protection law, rather than AI-specific rulemaking. That is changing. The 2023 interagency Request for Information on AI in financial services was a data-gathering exercise that precedes formal regulatory action. State-level AI legislation is advancing. The EU AI Act, while not directly applicable to US credit unions, is establishing global norms that will influence US regulatory thinking.

The direction of travel is toward more specific, more enforceable AI governance requirements. Institutions that have built programs aligned to the NIST AI RMF and the existing regulatory framework will find that alignment accommodates most foreseeable specific requirements without structural program changes. Those who have not will face a more demanding adaptation challenge when requirements harden.

Credit unions should monitor NCUA supervisory letters, interagency guidance releases, and state-level legislative developments for AI governance content on at least a semi-annual basis. The monitoring responsibility should be assigned to the ISPM, or the governance committee should review the compliance officer and the findings as part of the "emerging issues" standing agenda item established in Chapter 13.

Trend 2: Autonomous AI and Agentic Systems

The AI systems that most credit unions currently manage are primarily analytical: they produce recommendations, scores, classifications, and predictions that human staff act on. The AI systems arriving in the near-term environment are increasingly agentic: they take actions, execute workflows, and make decisions across multistep processes without per-step human review. An AI agent that autonomously manages a collections workflow, processes loan modifications, or handles member dispute resolution is not a recommendation engine that staff can override. It is an autonomous actor operating in the member relationship.

Agentic AI raises the governance stakes significantly. The Level 4 classification and the most stringent control requirements established in this book were designed with agentic systems in mind, but the governance program must evolve as agentic capabilities become more widely available through vendor platforms. The institution's risk appetite statement for autonomous AI, established in Chapter 16, will require periodic review as the boundary between decision support and autonomous action becomes more technically nuanced in available products.

The governance principle for agentic AI is the same one that governs Level 4 systems today: the institution must be able to explain, monitor, and intervene in autonomous AI actions affecting members, and must have defined escalation paths for when those systems behave outside their approved parameters. The governance infrastructure built for Level 4 systems is the foundation. The specific extension of that infrastructure to agentic use cases will be a significant governance program development in the next several years.

Trend 3: Consolidation of AI Governance Standards

The AI governance standards landscape is currently fragmented: NIST AI RMF, ISO/IEC 42001, EU AI Act, various industry frameworks, and emerging regulatory guidance all address overlapping territory with somewhat different structures, terminology, and emphasis. That fragmentation will consolidate over time as dominant standards emerge and regulatory requirements align with or reference them.

The NIST AI RMF is the most likely anchor standard for US financial institutions, given its regulatory endorsement and its design as a flexible, scalable framework rather than a prescriptive compliance checklist. Institutions that have built their programs against the AI RMF's four functions—GOVERN, MAP, MEASURE, and MANAGE—are well-positioned for the consolidation that follows. ISO/IEC 42001 is the management system standard most likely to become a certification benchmark; credit unions with ISO-aligned quality management systems should monitor its adoption trajectory.

As standards consolidate, the institutions that have invested in genuine program alignment rather than surface compliance will have an advantage. A program built to genuinely govern AI risk will map cleanly to whatever specific standard emerges. A program built to produce documentation artifacts for examination review will require a structural change when the standard changes.

Trend 4: Member Expectations and AI Literacy

Public awareness of AI in financial services is increasing. Members who currently ask occasional questions about whether AI was involved in a decision will develop more specific expectations about transparency, fairness, and control. The generation of members who are already fluent with AI tools in their personal lives will bring that fluency and expectations into their financial institution relationships. The transparency standard that feels proactive today—a plain-language responsible AI statement, a clear escalation pathway for AI-influenced decisions—will feel like a minimum expectation within a decade.

Credit unions that invest in member AI literacy, explaining in accessible terms how AI is used in their operations, what protections govern its use, and how members can exercise their rights, are building the member trust infrastructure that will distinguish them in an environment of increasing AI ubiquity. Members who understand and trust their institution's AI governance are members who have a positive reason to choose the credit union over a competitor with less transparent practices.

Trend 5: AI Governance As a Programmatic Discipline

AI governance is becoming a recognized programmatic discipline within financial institution risk management, distinct from general IT governance or information security program management. The ISPM or risk manager who built the institution's AI governance program is developing expertise that will be in demand across the sector. Industry associations, regulatory bodies, and peer institutions will increasingly look to practitioners with demonstrated AI governance experience to contribute to guidance development, examination preparation, and sector-wide standards work.

Credit union practitioners who have built genuine AI governance programs, who have navigated the real challenges of vendor opacity, shadow AI, resource constraints, and board communication that this book has addressed, have knowledge that cannot be produced by reading frameworks. That knowledge is worth contributing to the broader conversation. Participation in CUNA working groups, NASCUS technical committees, ISACA AI governance forums, and FS-ISAC AI risk-sharing channels converts individual program experience into sector-wide benefit and positions the credit union movement as a contributor to AI governance standards rather than a follower of them.

The AI Governance Program: From Construction to Maturity

Year 1—Construction: Inventory • Initial risk assessments • Policy foundation • Committee formation

Year 2—Operationalization: Monitoring program • Vendor due diligence integration • Board briefing cadence • Incident response capability

Year 3—Maturity: Program health self-assessment • Responsible AI audit • Forward planning against regulatory trends • Sector contribution

---

Ongoing—Continuous improvement: Each examination cycle, each incident, each new AI capability evaluated and governed makes the program stronger and more defensible.

A Closing Reflection

This book began on a Tuesday morning, and a VP of Lending noticed that loan decisions were moving faster than they used to. It ends with a governance program that has converted the quiet, unmanaged arrival of AI into a visible, governed, member-protective program that the institution can stand behind in an examination, present to its board with confidence, and explain to any member who asks.

The path between those two points was not technically complex. It did not require a large team, a significant budget, or specialized AI expertise. It required the willingness to look honestly at what was in the environment, the discipline to build governance structures that matched the actual risk, the communication skill to bring leadership and the board into a genuine engagement with the topic, and the values commitment to govern AI in a way that honored the member relationship rather than merely satisfying the regulatory minimum.

Those are practitioner capabilities. They are not scarce in the credit union movement; they are abundant in it. The ISPMs, risk managers, compliance officers, and technology leaders who read this book are already doing work that is harder, in many respects, than AI governance: managing information security programs, vendor portfolios, regulatory examinations, and institutional risk with teams that are small, budgets that are constrained, and high expectations. Adding AI governance to that portfolio is a meaningful expansion of scope. It is not a transformation of capability.

The credit union movement has always done more with less than its critics thought possible, in service of members who depended on it for financial access that was not available elsewhere. AI governance, done well, is an extension of that same commitment into the technological domain that will define financial services for the next generation. The institutions that govern it thoughtfully will be better positioned to serve their members, withstand examination scrutiny, and demonstrate that the cooperative model's values are not relics of a different era—they are governing principles that apply in this one as surely as in any that came before.

The governance program begins with an inventory. The program matures through consistent attention, honest self-assessment, and the willingness to improve in response to what monitoring, incidents, and examiners reveal. The program becomes excellent when the institution stops thinking of AI governance as a compliance obligation and starts thinking of it as an expression of what it is.

That is the program this book was written to help you build.

APPENDIX

Working Templates

AI Risk Management for Credit Unions

This appendix contains ten working templates that support the governance activities described throughout the book. Each template is designed to be adapted to the institution's specific environment, terminology, and governance structure. They are starting points, not final documents—the practitioner who uses them should review each for fit with their institution and adjust accordingly.

Templates are organized in the sequence in which the governance activities they support are introduced in the book, from inventory through board reporting.

A-1: AI System Inventory Template

A-2: AI Risk Assessment Template

A-3: Pre-deployment Evaluation Checklist

A-4: AI Vendor Due Diligence Questionnaire

A-5: AI Acceptable Use Policy Template

A-6: AI Governance Committee Charter Template

A-7: AI Incident Response Checklist

A-8: Annual Board AI Governance Briefing Template

A-9: AI Risk Assessment Worksheet

A-10: AI Vendor Risk Review Checklist

B. A. Salas, *AI Risk Management for Financial Institutions*,
https://doi.org/10.1007/979-8-8688-3353-3

A-1: AI System Inventory Template

Purpose: Maintain a current, comprehensive record of all AI systems operating within the institution's environment. The inventory is the foundational artifact of the AI governance program and must be reviewed and updated at least annually and whenever a new system is deployed or discovered.

Owner: ISPM | Review Cycle: Annual refresh + continuous intake | Committee Review: Quarterly summary

Field	Description/Guidance
System Name	Common name used by staff; include vendor product name if different
Vendor/Provider	Legal vendor name; "Internal" if built in-house; "Open Source" if applicable
Classification Level	Level 1, 2, 3, or 4 per AI Risk Classification Model (Chapter 4)
Primary Function	Plain-language description: What does this system do in our environment?
Business Unit Owner	Department or team that uses the system day-to-day
IT/Security Owner	Name the individual responsible for governance and monitoring
Member Data Involved	Yes/No. If yes, specify data categories (transaction, identity, behavioral, etc.)
Deployment Status	Active/Pilot/Inactive/Under Evaluation
Discovery Method	IT reviews/Departmental survey/Vendor portfolio review/Other

(*continued*)

Field	Description/Guidance
Date Added to Inventory	MM/DD/YYYY
Date of Last Risk Assessment	MM/DD/YYYY or "Not yet assessed."
Current Risk Disposition	Accepted/Conditionally Accepted/Under Remediation/ Pending Assessment
Open Remediation Items	Number of open items; reference the remediation log for details
Vendor Contract Status	Current/Renewal Due (date)/Month-to-Month/No Contract
AI Contract Provisions in Place	Yes/Partial/No—note which provisions are covered
Date of Last Vendor Review	MM/DD/YYYY we
Monitoring Frequency	Monthly/Quarterly/Annual/Not yet established
Notes	Relevant context: how the system was discovered, known gaps, pending actions

A-2: AI Risk Assessment Template

Purpose: Document the structured risk assessment for a single AI system. Complete one assessment record per system. Frequency: Level 1: Annual; Level 2: Semi-annual; Level 3/4: Quarterly or upon material change.

Owner: ISPM | Reviewed by: AI Governance Committee | Filed with: AI inventory record

System Identification	
System Name	
Vendor	
Classification Level	*Level 1/2/3/4*
Assessment Date	
Assessor	
Next Scheduled Assessment	
Prior Assessment Date	
Prior Residual Risk Rating	
Inherent Risk	
Classification Level Baseline	*Low (L1)/Moderate (L2)/High (L3)/Critical (L4)*
Data Sensitivity	*None/Low/Moderate/High—describe data categories involved*
Decision Impact	*None/Informational/Decision Support/Autonomous*
Model Opacity	*Transparent/Partially documented/Opaque*
Inherent Risk Rating	*Low/Moderate/High/Critical*
Inherent Risk Rationale	*Narrative explanation of rating*
Control Effectiveness	
Vendor Contract Provisions	*None/Partial/Comprehensive—note key provisions*

(*continued*)

Data Handling Controls	*None/Partial/Comprehensive*
Human Oversight Mechanisms	*None/Advisory/Required Review*
Monitoring Program	*None/Established/Active with defined thresholds*
Staff Training/AUP Coverage	*None/Informal/Documented Policy*
Incident Response Coverage	*Not Addressed/Partial/Fully Covered*
Overall Control Effectiveness	*Weak/Moderate/Strong*
Control Effectiveness Rationale	*Narrative explanation; note any design or operational gaps*
Residual Risk and Disposition	
Residual Risk Rating	*Low/Moderate/High/Critical*
Residual Risk Rationale	*Narrative: identify irreducible risks (e.g., vendor opacity, floor)*
Risk Disposition	*Accept/Accept Conditionally/Mitigate/Transfer/Avoid*
ConditionsRemediation Required	*List specific actions required; assign owner and due date*
Risk Appetite Alignment	*Within Appetite/Exceeds Appetite (requires escalation)*
Committee Review Date	
Committee Decision	*Accepted/Escalated/Returned for Additional Assessment*

(*continued*)

Responsible AI assessment (Level 3/4)	
Fairness	*Outcome analysis conducted: Yes/No/Pending Finding*
Transparency	*Member explanation capability: Adequate/Inadequate/N/A*
Human Dignity	*Human review mechanisms: In place/Partial/Absent*
Accountability	*Incident remediation record: Clean/Open items (reference log)*

A-3: Pre-deployment Evaluation Checklist

Purpose: Ensure consistent evaluation of AI systems before they are deployed or approved for continued use. Complete before any Level 3 or Level 4 deployment. Use the lightweight version for Level 1 and Level 2 (sections 1 and 2 only). Approval authority: Level 1/2: ISPM; Level 3: Risk Committee; Level 4: Executive with Board Notification.

Section 1: Purpose and Function		
☐	The system's purpose is clearly documented and consistent with the vendor's product description	*Pass/Fail/N/A*
☐	Intended users and use cases are defined and limited to the approved scope	*Pass/Fail/N/A*
☐	AI/ML capabilities are specifically identified (not just inferred from product marketing)	*Pass/Fail/N/A*

(*continued*)

☐	Classification level has been assigned using the AI Risk Classification Model	*Pass/Fail/N/A*
☐	The business unit owner has confirmed the use case and accepted governance responsibilities	*Pass/Fail/N/A*

Section 2: Data Handling

☐	Data categories that the system ingests have been identified and classified	*Pass/Fail/N/A*
☐	Member data exposure has been confirmed or ruled out	*Pass/Fail/N/A*
☐	Vendor data retention period has been documented	*Pass/Fail/N/A*
☐	Prohibition on training vendor models on member data is confirmed or pending negotiation	*Pass/Fail/N/A*
☐	Sub-processors have been identified and disclosed	*Pass/Fail/N/A*
☐	Data handling terms are compatible with GLBA Safeguards Rule obligations	*Pass/Fail/N/A*

Section 3: Model Transparency (Level 3/4)

☐	The vendor has provided model documentation or a technical summary	*Pass/Fail/N/A*
☐	Model validation documentation is on file	*Pass/Fail/N/A*

(*continued*)

☐	Model limitations and known failure modes are documented	*Pass/Fail/N/A*
☐	Fair lending/disparate impact testing has been conducted, and the results are on file	*Pass/Fail/N/A*
☐	Adverse action explanation capability has been confirmed	*Pass/Fail / N/A*
☐	The vendor notification process for material model changes has been established	*Pass/Fail/N/A*

Section 4: Vendor Accountability (Level 3/4)

☐	Vendor contracts include AI-specific data handling provisions	*Pass/Fail/N/A*
☐	The model change notification clause is in the contract or pending negotiation	*Pass/Fail/N/A*
☐	Audit rights covering AI performance metrics are established	*Pass/Fail/N/A*
☐	Vendor SLA covers AI-specific performance in addition to system availability	*Pass/Fail/N/A*
☐	Vendor security assessments have included AI-specific questions	*Pass/Fail/N/A*
☐	Sub-processor contractual obligations flow through to the primary vendor agreement	*Pass/Fail/N/A*

(*continued*)

Section 5: Operational Readiness (Level 3/4)

☐	Staff training requirements have been defined and scheduled	*Pass/Fail/N/A*
☐	Human oversight mechanisms (review, challenge, override) are designed and documented	*Pass/Fail/N/A*
☐	A manual fallback procedure exists if the AI system is unavailable	*Pass/Fail/N/A*
☐	Performance baselines have been documented for ongoing monitoring	*Pass/Fail/N/A*
☐	Monitoring frequency and escalation criteria have been defined	*Pass/Fail/N/A*
☐	The incident response procedure covers this system's classification and incident types	*Pass/Fail/N/A*
☐	Risk assessment has been completed, and the governance committee has reviewed it	*Pass/Fail/N/A*
Evaluation Outcome	☐ Approved for deployment ☐ Conditionally approved ☐ Not approved	*Approver:* ______________ *Date:*____________

A-4: AI Vendor Due Diligence Questionnaire

Purpose: Evaluate AI-specific risks in vendor relationships. Send to vendors whose platforms include AI or ML capabilities. Use the responses to complete the vendor risk section of the AI Risk Assessment (A-2) and to conduct contract negotiations. Retain responses as part of the vendor risk file.

Data Exposure Risk	
Q1. Does your platform use AI or machine learning in any component? If yes, describe which components and their functions.	*Vendor response:*
Q2. Does your AI system process, store, or transmit customer financial data? If yes, specify data categories and processing locations.	*Vendor response:*
Q3. Does your organization retain customer data used in AI processing after the transaction is complete? If yes, for how long and under what data governance controls?	*Vendor response:*
Q4. Does your organization use customer data, or outputs derived from customer data, to train or improve your AI models? If yes, describe the process and any opt-out mechanisms available to customers.	*Vendor response:*
Q5. Are third-party sub-processors involved in any AI data processing? If yes, identify them and describe their role and your contractual obligations to them.	*Vendor response:*
Model Transparency	
Q6. Has your AI model been independently validated? If yes, summarize the validation scope, methodology, and findings.	*Vendor response:*
Q7. What are the known limitations of your AI model, and under what conditions does it perform below its documented baseline?	*Vendor response:*

(continued)

Q8. Has your AI model been tested for bias, disparate impact, or differential performance across demographic segments? Provide the testing method and results.	*Vendor response:*
Q9. How does your system generate explanations for adverse decisions produced by or influenced by the AI model?	*Vendor response:*
Q10. What is your process for notifying customers when the AI model has been materially retrained, or its behavior has changed significantly?	*Vendor response:*

Operational Dependence

Q11. What is your SLA for AI-specific performance metrics (accuracy, availability of AI features) versus general system availability?	*Vendor response:*
Q12. How do you communicate AI system degradation that does not rise to the level of a full outage?	*Vendor response:*
Q13. What manual fallback capabilities does your platform support if the AI component is unavailable?	*Vendor response:*
Q14. Describe your business continuity and disaster recovery capabilities specific to AI system components.	*Vendor response:*

Regulatory Impact

Q15. Has your AI system been reviewed for compliance with SR 11-7 model risk management guidance? If yes, provide documentation.	*Vendor response:*
Q16. Has your organization received any regulatory inquiry, examination findings, or enforcement action related to AI system performance or governance? If yes, describe.	*Vendor response:*

(*continued*)

Q17. Does your AI system affect credit decisions, fraud determinations, or other actions that trigger ECOA, FCRA, or UDAAP obligations? If yes, how does your system support customer adverse action notification?	*Vendor response:*
Q18. Describe your AI-specific security controls, including adversarial attack monitoring, prompt injection protections (if applicable), and software supply chain security practices.	*Vendor response:*

A-5: AI Acceptable Use Policy Template

Note: Italicized bracketed text indicates fields to be completed by the institution. Legal counsel should review this template before adoption. Replace [INSTITUTION NAME] throughout.

1. Purpose and Scope

This policy establishes the acceptable use of artificial intelligence (AI) tools and systems by [INSTITUTION NAME] staff. It applies to all employees, contractors, and third parties acting on behalf of the institution who use AI tools in their work, including tools provided by [INSTITUTION NAME], approved vendor platforms with AI capabilities, and any externally available AI tools accessed using institution equipment or data.

2. Approved AI Tools

The following AI tools have been reviewed and approved for institutional use. Use is permitted within the scope and data restrictions noted:

Approved Tools Register (maintained by ISPM—current as of policy review date)

Tool Name	Approved Use Case	Data Restrictions	Approved Users
[Tool 1]	[Use case]	[Restrictions]	[User group]
[Tool 2]	[Use case]	[Restrictions]	[User group]

Note: This register is updated as tools are approved or retired. The current version is available from ISPM.

3. Data Handling Restrictions

Staff must not input, upload, or paste the following data categories into any AI tool that has not been explicitly approved for that data type, regardless of whether the tool appears on the approved list:

- Member Social Security numbers, tax identification numbers, or government-issued identification numbers.
- Member account numbers, routing numbers, or full payment card data.
- Member non-public personal information (NPI) as defined under GLBA, unless the tool has been specifically approved for NPI processing.
- Internal financial projections, strategic plans, or confidential board materials.
- Employee personal information, compensation data, or performance records.

- Any data subject to a confidentiality agreement or legal hold.

When in doubt about whether a data category is permitted for a specific tool, staff should contact [ISPM/IT Security] before using the tool with that data.

4. Requesting Evaluation of a New AI Tool

Staff who wish to use an AI tool not on the approved list must submit a tool evaluation request to [ISPM/IT Security] before using the tool. Requests should include the tool name, vendor, intended use case, and data categories involved. The ISPM will provide a first response within five business days. Staff must not use an unapproved tool while an evaluation is pending.

5. Disclosure Obligation

Staff who are currently using an AI tool that has not been through the evaluation process must disclose it to [ISPM/IT Security] within [30 days of this policy's effective date/within 30 days of becoming aware of this obligation]. Disclosure will be treated as a governance activity, not a disciplinary matter, unless the use involved deliberate circumvention of a known policy requirement or involved data categories prohibited under Section 3.

6. Consequence Framework

Staff who use AI tools in deliberate violation of this policy—including using tools after being informed they are not approved, or processing prohibited data categories after being trained on this policy—may be subject to disciplinary action up to and including termination, consistent with [INSTITUTION NAME]'s employee handbook and HR policies.

7. Policy Review

This policy will be reviewed annually by the ISPM and updated as needed to reflect changes in the institution's AI environment, approved tools, or regulatory requirements. Material updates will be communicated to all staff. Effective date: [DATE]. Policy owner: [ISPM NAME/TITLE].

A-6: AI Governance Committee Charter Template

Note: Executive leadership or the board should approve this charter, as appropriate to the institution's governance structure. It may be incorporated as an appendix to the AI Governance Policy or maintained as a standalone governance document.

1. Purpose

The [INSTITUTION NAME] AI Governance Committee ("Committee") is established to provide institutional oversight of the credit union's artificial intelligence governance program. The Committee ensures that AI systems are deployed, managed, and monitored in a manner consistent with the institution's risk appetite, regulatory obligations, and member-first values.

2. Authority

The Committee is authorized by [Executive Leadership/Board of Directors] to review and approve AI deployments at Level 3 and Level 4 of the AI Risk Classification Model; to review and formally accept or escalate risk assessment findings; to oversee the AI governance program's health and recommend improvements; and to prepare and deliver AI governance briefings to executive leadership and the board.

3. Membership

Core Members (required for quorum): Information Security Program Manager (Chair or Co-Chair); Risk Manager; Compliance Officer; [Chief Information Officer/Technology Leader]; [Legal Counsel, if available].

Optional Members (engaged as needed): Data Governance Lead; Internal Audit; Business Unit Representatives for specific agenda items.

Quorum requires [3 of 4/a majority of] Core Members to be present for decisions. Decisions are documented in meeting minutes and require [unanimous/majority] agreement.

4. Meeting Cadence

The Committee meets quarterly on a schedule established at the beginning of each calendar year. Out-of-cycle meetings may be convened by the Committee Chair for: Level 4 deployment approvals; significant AI incidents requiring Committee review; material regulatory guidance requiring program response. Meeting minutes are produced within five business days of each meeting.

5. Reporting

The Committee reports to executive leadership on a quarterly basis and to the board of directors on an annual basis at a minimum. The Chair is responsible for coordinating the production of briefing materials. Significant AI incidents meeting the policy's board notification threshold are reported to the board chair within [5 business days] of the Committee's review.

6. Charter Review

This charter is reviewed annually as part of the AI governance policy review cycle. Amendments require approval from [executive leadership/ the board]. Effective date: [DATE]. Approved by: [NAME/TITLE].

A-7: AI Incident Response Checklist

Purpose: Guide the response to an AI-related incident from initial detection through post-incident review. Complete in sequence. All checked items should be documented with the date, time, and responsible party. This checklist supplements the institution's standard incident response plan.

Phase 1: Detection and Classification (Target: within 1 hour)

☐	Incident reported/detected. Document source, date, and time.	*By:*____________ *Date:*________
☐	Preliminary facts gathered: which AI system is involved and what anomaly has been observed.	*By:*____________ *Date:*________

(*continued*)

☐	Incident classified: ☐ Performance Anomaly ☐ Data Incident ☐ Member Harm ☐ Security Incident	*By:* ______________ *Date:* _________
☐	ISPM notified (if not already leading the response).	*By:* ______________ *Date:* _________
☐	Vendor notified of anomaly and response timeline requested.	*By:* ______________ *Date:* _________

Phase 2: Containment (Target: within 4 hours)

☐	AI system suspension decision made: ☐ Suspend ☐ Continue with oversight ☐ No action required	*By:* ______________ *Date:* _________
☐	Suspension rationale documented.	*By:* ______________ *Date:* _________
☐	Affected business units are notified, and the manual workflow is activated if the AI is suspended.	*By:* ______________ *Date:* _________
☐	Evidence preserved: logs, outputs, and decision records for the affected period.	*By:* ______________ *Date:* _________
☐	No evidence modification or deletion without legal/compliance approval.	*By:* ______________ *Date:* _________

Phase 3: Impact Assessment (Target: within 48 hours for data incidents)

☐	Time window of anomalous behavior identified.	*By:* ______________ *Date:* _________
☐	Members affected during the window identified from decision/transaction records.	*By:* ______________ *Date:* _________
☐	Nature of impact assessed for each affected member: ☐ No impact ☐ Potential impact ☐ Confirmed harm	*By:* ______________ *Date:* _________

(continued)

☐ For data incidents: GLBA notification assessment checklist completed.	*By:* ____________ *Date:* ________
☐ GLBA notification threshold determination documented: ☐ Threshold met ☐ Threshold not met	*By:* ____________ *Date:* ________
☐ For member harm incidents: remediation options identified for each affected member.	*By:* ____________ *Date:* ________

Phase 4: Notification and Escalation

☐ The Governance Committee Chair was notified per the escalation protocol.	*By:* ____________ *Date:* ________
☐ Full Committee engaged if required by escalation criteria.	*By:* ____________ *Date:* ________
☐ GLBA notification filed with FTC if threshold met (within 30 days of discovery).	*By:* ____________ *Date:* ________
☐ Affected members will be contacted individually if member harm is confirmed.	*By:* ____________ *Date:* ________
☐ Member remediation offered and documented.	*By:* ____________ *Date:* ________
☐ Board notification is made if the policy threshold is met.	*By:* ____________ *Date:* ________
☐ Regulatory notification is made if required beyond GLBA (NCUA, state regulator).	*By:* ____________ *Date:* ________

(continued)

Phase 5: Resolution and Post-Incident Review

☐	AI system restored to operation (or replacement decision made) with documented approval.	*By:* ________ *Date:* ________
☐	Vendor corrective action confirmed and documented.	*By:* ________ *Date:* ________
☐	Post-incident review conducted within 30 days of resolution.	*By:* ________ *Date:* ________
☐	Root cause identified and documented.	*By:* ________ *Date:* ________
☐	Control gaps were identified and entered into the remediation tracking system.	*By:* ________ *Date:* ________
☐	Program improvements defined, assigned, and scheduled.	*By:* ________ *Date:* ________
☐	The incident report was finalized and presented to the Risk Committee.	*By:* ________ *Date:* ________
☐	Incident records are archived in the AI governance documentation file.	*By:* ________ *Date:* ________

A-8: Annual Board AI Governance Briefing Template

Purpose: Structure the annual board AI governance briefing for consistent, substantive engagement. Target: 12–15 minutes presentation, 5–10 minutes for questions. Slide content guidance is provided below for each of the five recommended slides. Adapt the language to the institution's culture and the board's communication style.

Slide 1	**What AI is doing in our institution**

List each active AI system by its member-facing function (not its technical name):

- *[System A]: Analyzes member transactions to identify potential fraud*
- *[System B]: Reviews loan applications and produces a risk recommendation for our loan officers*
- *[System C]: Routes member service inquiries to the appropriate support channel*
- *[System D]: Assists staff in drafting member correspondence*

Total active AI systems: [N] | Systems added since last briefing: [N] | Systems retired: [N]

Slide 2	**Our AI Risk Posture**

Inventory summary by classification level:

Level 1 (Informational): [N] systems • Level 2 (Operational): [N] systems

Level 3 (Decision Support): [N] systems • Level 4 (Autonomous): [N] systems

Risk assessment status:

Current (assessed within required cycle): [N] • Due for reassessment: [N]

Residual risk summary: Low: [N] • Moderate: [N] • High: [N] • Critical: [N]

Trend vs. prior year: [Improving/Stable/Deteriorating]—brief narrative explanation

(*continued*)

Slide 3	Significant Risks and Management Responses

Present the top 2–3 high or critical residual risk items. For each:
Risk: [Plain-language description of the risk and potential member impact]
Status: [What management is doing about it]
Timeline: [When remediation is expected to be complete]
Example: "Our lending AI vendor has not provided demographic outcome testing results.
This creates fair lending exposure. We are requiring this documentation as a condition.
of our contract renewal in Q [X]. Deadline: [DATE]."

Slide 4	Program Health

Governance committee: [N] meetings held this year • [N] deployments reviewed • [N] incidents reviewed
Monitoring: AI monitoring report produced monthly • [N] exceptions flagged • [N] escalated
Policy currency: AI governance policy last reviewed [DATE] • [Current/Update pending]
Examination readiness: [No findings/One MRA addressed/Clean examination]—brief note
Forward agenda: [Key program priorities for the coming year in 2–3 bullet points]

(continued)

Slide 5 **What We Need from the Board**

Be explicit. Choose one of the following and prepare the appropriate motion or acknowledgment:

Option A: Information only:

"No board action is required. This briefing is provided for your awareness and to document it.

The board's annual engagement with AI governance, as required by our governance policy."

Option B: Policy adoption/reaffirmation:

"We are asking the board to formally adopt the updated AI Governance Policy, which was

last amended to [describe the change]. A copy has been provided in your board packet."

Option C: Risk appetite reaffirmation:

"We are asking the board to reaffirm the institution's AI risk appetite statement,
which was last adopted on [DATE]. No material changes are proposed at this time."

Suggested Board Minutes Framework (A-8 Supplement)

AI Governance Briefing: Suggested Minutes Language

The [Chief Information Security/Risk] Officer presented the annual AI governance briefing.

The presentation described [N] active AI systems operating in the institution, summarized the current risk posture, including [N] systems at high or critical residual risk, and outlined the governance program's forward agenda for [YEAR].

Board members asked questions regarding [summarize 1–2 key questions and management responses].

The board [noted the briefing for informational purposes/formally adopted the updated AI Governance Policy/reaffirmed the institution's AI risk appetite statement] by [unanimous vote/consensus]. No further board action was required at this time.

A-9: AI Risk Assessment Worksheet

Purpose: A working tool to guide the assessor through the analytical steps of an AI risk assessment. Use this worksheet to develop your ratings. Transfer the final ratings and rationale to the AI Risk Assessment Template (A-2) for the formal record. This worksheet does not need to be retained as a permanent document; it is a scratchpad, not a record.

How to use: Work through each section in sequence. Circle or highlight the descriptor that best matches the system being assessed. At the end of each section, record the rating and your supporting rationale. The worksheet is designed so that a well-supported rating can be reached in 30–45 minutes for Level 1/2 systems and 60–90 minutes for Level 3/4 systems.

STEP 1: Inherent Risk Scoring

Factor	Score Descriptors—circle the one that best fits	Score (1–4) + Rationale
Classification Level *What level does this system operate at based on its function?*	**1—Low**: Level 1: Informational only. No member decisions. Internal staff tool. **2—Moderate**: Level 2: Operational support. May touch member data. Staff can override. **3—High**: Level 3: Informs consequential member decisions directly. **4—Critical**: Level 4: Autonomous. Acts on member accounts without per-decision review.	*Score:___ Rationale:*

(*continued*)

Data Sensitivity *What categories of data does this system process?*	**1—Low**: No member data. Internal operational data only. **2—Moderate**: Member contact information or general account metadata. No financial details. **3—High**: Member financial data, transaction history, or behavioral profiles. **4—Critical**: Identity documents, biometrics, or highly sensitive member financial profiles.	*Score:* ___	*Rationale:*
Decision Impact *How directly does this system's output affect member outcomes?*	**1—Low**: The output is informational. No connection to member-facing decisions. **2—Moderate**: Output supports operational efficiency. Indirect member impact. **3—High:** Output directly informs credit, fraud, or account decisions. **4—Critical**: Output triggers automated account actions with no human review.	*Score:* ___	*Rationale:*

(*continued*)

Model Opacity *How well can the institution explain how the system produces its outputs?*	**1—Low**: Fully transparent. Logic is rule-based or fully documented. **2—Moderate**: Vendor provides meaningful documentation. Limitations are disclosed. **3—High**: Limited documentation. General model type known, but logic opaque. **4—Critical**: Black box. The vendor cannot or will not explain how the outputs are produced.	*Score:*___ *Rationale:*

Inherent Risk Rating: Average the four factor scores and round to the nearest whole number. Map to: **1 = Low • 2 = Moderate • 3 = High • 4 = Critical**
*Rating:*____________

(*continued*)

STEP 2: Control Effectivness Scoring

Control Domain—Assessment Question	Weak/Moderate/Strong—circle one + evidence note
Vendor Contract Provisions *Does the vendor contract include AI-specific data handling, change notification, and audit terms?*	○ **Weak**: No AI-specific provisions. Standard contract only. ○ **Moderate**: Some provisions present but incomplete (e.g., data handling covered, no change notification). ○ **Strong:** Comprehensive: data handling, training restrictions, change notification, and audit rights are all present. *Evidence on file:* ___________ ____________________
Data Handling Controls *Are there institutional controls governing what member data flows into this system?*	○ **Weak**: No data handling controls. Member data used without restriction. ○ **Moderate:** Basic controls exist (e.g., AUP mentions this system) but are not fully enforced or verified. ○ **Strong**: Defined data categories approved. Purpose limitations enforced. Verified against actual usage. *Evidence on file:* ___________ ____________________

(continued)

Human Oversight Mechanisms *Can staff review, challenge, and override AI outputs before they affect members?*	○ **Weak**: No human review. The system acts autonomously on member accounts. ○ **Moderate**: Human review exists but is advisory only or inconsistently applied. ○ **Strong**: Mandatory human review of all AI-influenced member decisions. Override process documented and used. *Evidence on file:* ___________ ______________________
Monitoring Program *Is there an active monitoring process that would detect performance degradation or behavioral drift?*	○ **Weak**: No monitoring. Performance issues would surface only through incidents or complaints. ○ **Moderate:** Vendor-provided reporting reviewed periodically. No institution-side outcome tracking. ○ **Strong**: Active monitoring with defined baselines, escalation thresholds, and institution-side outcome analysis. *Evidence on file:* ___________ ______________________

(*continued*)

Staff Training and AUP Coverage *Do staff understand how to use this system appropriately and what data restrictions apply?*	○ **Weak:** No training. No AUP coverage for this system. ○ **Moderate**: Training provided at onboarding. AUP covers AI generally, but not this system specifically. ○ **Strong:** Role-specific training. System covered explicitly in AUP. Annual refresher documented. *Evidence on file:* ___________ _______________________
Incident Response Coverage *Is this system covered in incident response procedures with specific scenarios and response paths?*	○ **Weak:** Not addressed in the incident response plan. ○ **Moderate**: General IT incident procedures apply, but no AI-specific scenarios or response paths are defined. ○ **Strong:** AI-specific incident scenarios documented. Response paths tested in a tabletop exercise. *Evidence on file:* ___________ _______________________

Overall Control Effectiveness: Review the pattern of ratings above. The majority Weak = Weak overall. Mixed = Moderate. Majority Strong = Strong. *Rating:* ___________ *Key gaps to note:*

(*continued*)

STEP 3: Residual Risk Determination

Use the matrix below to determine Residual Risk from your Inherent Risk rating and Control Effectiveness rating:

	Control Effectiveness: Weak	Control Effectiveness: Moderate	Control Effectiveness: Strong
Inherent Risk: Low	Moderate	Low	Low
Inherent Risk: Moderate	High	Moderate	Low–Moderate
Inherent Risk: High	Critical	High	Moderate
Inherent Risk: Critical	Critical	Critical	High

STEP 4: Risk Disposition Decision

Accept	Residual risk is within appetite. No remediation required. Document the rationale and schedule the next assessment.
Accept Conditionally	Residual risk is above appetite, but the system has operational value. Define specific remediation actions with owners and due dates. Re-assess at the next cycle.
Mitigate	Implement additional controls to reduce residual risk before or during continued use. Define milestones.
Transfer	Shift risk through vendor contractual obligations, insurance, or third-party monitoring arrangements.
Avoid	Residual risk exceeds appetite and cannot be adequately reduced. Discontinued use of the system.

*Selected disposition:*________________ *Rationale:*___________________________

___________________________ *Owner:*________________ *Due:*_____________

A-10: AI Vendor Risk Review Checklist

Purpose: An internal evaluation tool used after vendor responses to the AI Vendor Due Diligence Questionnaire (A-4) have been received. Use this checklist to synthesize what the vendor said into a structured risk rating per category. The ratings produced here feed directly into the vendor risk section of the AI Risk Assessment (A-2) and should be retained in the vendor risk file alongside the questionnaire responses.

How to use: For each item, mark the finding based on the vendor's response and your evaluation. At the end of each category, assign a category risk rating. Transfer the four category ratings to A-2 under Control Effectiveness for vendor-side controls.

Category 1: Data Exposure Risk

Finding/Evaluation Point	Vendor Response Assessment	Follow-up needed?
Vendor confirmed whether the AI system processes member data	Yes, clearly ✓ / Partial ○ / Not addressed ○ / Declined to answer ○	○ Yes ○ No
The vendor disclosed all data categories processed by the AI system	Yes, clearly ✓ / Partial ○ / Not addressed ○ / Declined to answer ○	○ Yes ○ No
Vendor disclosed data retention periods and controls	Yes, clearly ✓ / Partial ○ / Not addressed ○ / Declined to answer ○	○ Yes ○ No
Vendor confirmed member data is not used for model training (or provided opt-out)	Confirmed ✓ / Used with opt-out ○ / Used without opt-out ○ / Not disclosed ○	○ Yes ○ No

(continued)

All sub-processors involved in AI data handling are disclosed	All disclosed ✓ / Partially disclosed ○ / Not disclosed ○ / No sub-processors confirmed ○	○ Yes ○ No
The vendor's data handling terms are compatible with GLBA obligations	Compatible ✓ / Requires negotiation ○ / Incompatible ○ / Unable to assess ○	○ Yes ○ No

Category 1 Risk Rating: ○ Low ○ Moderate ○ High ○ Critical Key concern:

Category 2: Model Transparency

Finding/Evaluation Point	**Vendor Response Assessment**	**Follow-up Needed?**
Vendor provided model documentation or technical summary	Comprehensive ✓ / Summary only ○ / Marketing material only ○ / None provided ○	○ Yes ○ No
Independent validation has been conducted, and documentation is available	Provided ✓ / Exists but not shared ○ / Not conducted ○ / Unknown ○	○ Yes ○ No
Model limitations and known failure modes are documented	Documented ✓ / Partially ○ / Not documented ○ / Declined to disclose ○	○ Yes ○ No
Fair lending/disparate impact testing has been conducted	Conducted, results provided ✓ / Conducted, results withheld ○ / Not conducted ○ / Unknown ○	○ Yes ○ No

(continued)

Testing was conducted on data comparable to this institution's member population	Institution-specific ✓ / National dataset ○ / Not disclosed ○ / Not applicable ○	○ Yes ○ No
The vendor has a defined process for notifying customers of material model changes	Defined, contractable ✓ / Informal process ○ / No process ○ / Unknown ○	○ Yes ○ No
Vendors can support adverse action explanation requirements for AI-influenced decisions	Supported ✓ / Partially supported ○ / Not supported ○ / Not applicable ○	○ Yes ○ No

Category 2 Risk Rating: ○ Low ○ Moderate ○ High ○ Critical Key concern:

Category 3: Operational Dependence

Finding/Evaluation Point	**Vendor Response Assessment**	**Follow-up Needed?**
Vendor SLA covers AI-specific performance metrics (not just system availability)	Yes ✓ / Availability only ○ / No SLA for AI components ○ / Unknown ○	○ Yes ○ No
The vendor has a defined process for communicating AI degradation short of a full outage	Defined ✓ / Ad hoc only ○ / No process ○ / Unknown ○	○ Yes ○ No
The platform supports manual fallback if the AI component is unavailable	Full fallback ✓ / Partial fallback ○ / No fallback ○ / Unknown ○	○ Yes ○ No

(*continued*)

Vendor's business continuity plan addresses AI-specific component recovery	Documented ✓ / General BCP only ○ / Not addressed ○ / Unknown ○	○ Yes ○ No
The institution's own BCP reflects dependency on this AI system	Yes ✓ / Not yet updated ○ / No ○	○ Yes ○ No

Category 3 Risk Rating: ○ Low ○ Moderate ○ High ○ Critical Key concern:

Category 4: Regulatory Impact

Finding/Evaluation Point	Vendor Response Assessment	Follow-up needed?
The vendor has reviewed the AI system against SR 11-7 model risk management expectations	Reviewed, documented ✓ / Informal review ○ / Not reviewed ○ / Unknown ○	○ Yes ○ No
The vendor has received no regulatory findings or enforcement actions related to this AI system	Confirmed clean ✓ / Minor findings only ○ / Material findings ○ / Not disclosed ○	○ Yes ○ No
Vendor AI system supports ECOA/ FCRA adverse action notice requirements	Supported ✓ / Partial support ○ / Not supported ○ / Not applicable ○	○ Yes ○ No
The vendor has described AI-specific security controls (adversarial monitoring, prompt injection, supply chain)	Described ✓ / General security only ○ / Not addressed ○ / Declined to disclose ○	○ Yes ○ No
The vendor is willing to include AI-specific provisions in contract negotiations	Yes, engaged ✓ / Partial willingness ○ / Standard terms only ○ / Declined ○	○ Yes ○ No

(*continued*)

Category 4 Risk Rating: ○ Low ○ Moderate ○ High ○ Critical Key concern:

OVERALL VENDOR AI RISK SUMMARY

Vendor Name	
AI System/Platform Reviewed	
Review Date	
Reviewer	
Category 1—Data Exposure Risk	○ Low ○ Moderate ○ High ○ Critical
Category 2—Model Transparency	○ Low ○ Moderate ○ High ○ Critical
Category 3—Operational Dependence	○ Low ○ Moderate ○ High ○ Critical
Category 4—Regulatory Impact	○ Low ○ Moderate ○ High ○ Critical
Overall Vendor AI Risk Rating	○ Low ○ Moderate ○ High ○ Critical (highest of four categories, or judgment if mixed)
Contract Provisions Required	*List provisions to negotiate based on the findings above:*
Follow-up Items Outstanding	*List items marked 'Yes' above requiring vendor response before risk assessment is completed:*
Recommended Risk Disposition	○ Proceed with contract ○ Proceed with conditions ○ Do not proceed

These templates are starting points. Every institution's AI environment, governance structure, and regulatory profile is somewhat different, and the practitioner who uses these templates should review each for fit and adjust accordingly. Templates should be reviewed annually alongside the AI governance policy and updated to reflect changes in the institution's AI inventory, governance structure, and regulatory requirements.

Practitioners who develop significant improvements to these templates based on their implementation experience are encouraged to share them with the broader credit union AI governance community through CUNA, NASCUS, ISACA credit union chapters, or FS-ISAC working groups. The collective improvement of governance practices across the sector strengthens every institution within it.

Glossary

The following terms are used throughout this book in specific technical or governance senses. Definitions reflect their meaning as applied in the credit union AI governance context.

Agentic AI: AI systems that take sequential actions and execute multistep workflows autonomously, without per-step human review. Distinct from decision support AI in that the system acts rather than recommends. Addressed in Chapter 18 as an emerging governance challenge requiring Level 4 classification and controls.

Adversarial attack: A deliberate attempt to manipulate an AI model by crafting inputs designed to produce incorrect outputs. In financial services, it most commonly manifests as boundary probing—systematically testing a fraud detection model's thresholds to identify where detection fails, then operating inside that boundary. See Chapter 10.

AI Governance Committee: The formally chartered, cross-functional body responsible for institutional oversight of AI risk decisions, deployments, and program health. Core membership includes Information Security, Risk Management, Compliance, and Technology Leadership. Introduced in Chapter 12; operations are detailed in Chapter 13.

B. A. Salas, *AI Risk Management for Financial Institutions*,
https://doi.org/10.1007/979-8-8688-3353-3

AI Governance Pyramid: The five-layer governance model introduced in Chapter 2 provides the structural framework for this book. Layers from foundation to apex: Layer 1: AI Systems; Layer 2: Operational Controls; Layer 3: AI Risk Management; Layer 4: AI Governance Program; Layer 5: Strategic Oversight.

AI Risk Classification Model: The four-level framework introduced in Chapter 4 for categorizing AI systems by risk profile and calibrating the depth of evaluation and oversight required: Level 1 (Informational/Low), Level 2 (Operational/ Moderate), Level 3 (Decision Support/High), Level 4 (Autonomous/Critical).

AI Vendor Risk Evaluation Model: The four-category due diligence framework introduced in Chapter 6 for assessing AI-specific risks in vendor relationships: Category 1: Data Exposure Risk; Category 2: Model Transparency; Category 3: Operational Dependence; Category 4: Regulatory Impact.

Algorithmic bias: The systematic production of different outcomes for individuals based on protected class characteristics or proxies for those characteristics by an AI model, even without explicit discriminatory intent. Creates fair lending exposure under ECOA, FHA, and UDAAP. See Chapters 6, 9, and 17.

Behavioral monitoring: The ongoing practice of tracking whether an AI system is being used in ways consistent with its governance approvals and intended purpose. Distinct from performance monitoring (is the system working correctly?) and governance monitoring (is the program operating has designed?). See Chapter 11.

Conditional acceptance: A risk disposition in which the institution accepts residual risk on a time-limited basis, contingent on specific remediation actions with defined owners and due dates documented in the risk assessment record. The most common disposition for AI systems is delivering operational value with identified governance gaps. See Chapter 5.

Control effectiveness: An assessment of whether a governance control reduces the risk it targets. Design effectiveness evaluates whether the control is designed appropriately; operational effectiveness evaluates whether it functions as designed in practice. Evidence of both is required for a meaningful control assessment. See Chapter 14.

Data exposure risk: The risk that vendor AI capabilities create unauthorized or unintended access to, retention of, or use of member data. One of the four categories in the AI Vendor Risk Evaluation Model. Most directly implicates GLBA Safeguards Rule obligations. See Chapters 6 and 9.

Defensibility: The standard against which AI governance programs are assessed by examiners: a documented, good-faith program proportionate to the institution's size, complexity, and risk profile.

Not synonymous with perfection. A candid gap analysis with a remediation plan is more defensible than silence. See Chapters 1 and 3.

Disparate impact: A pattern of AI-assisted decisions that produces systematically different outcomes for protected class groups, regardless of whether discrimination was intended. Testing for disparate impact is a prerequisite for responsible AI deployment in lending and account management. See Chapters 6, 9, and 17.

ECOA (Equal Credit Opportunity Act): Federal law prohibiting discrimination in credit decisions based on race, color, religion, national origin, sex, marital status, age, or receipt of public assistance. Applies to AI-assisted lending decisions and requires meaningful adverse action notices when AI contributes to a denial. See Chapters 3 and 9.

FFIEC (Federal Financial Institutions Examination Council): An interagency body that establishes uniform examination standards for federal financial institution regulators, including the NCUA. The FFIEC IT Examination Handbook governs technology governance, vendor management, audit, and development and acquisition processes applicable to AI systems. See Chapter 3.

GLBA Safeguards Rule: Requirements under the Gramm-Leach-Bliley Act, administered by the FTC, governing how financial institutions protect customer financial information. The

2021 amendments strengthened data protection requirements. Applies to all AI data handling, including vendor AI systems processing member data. See Chapters 3 and 9.

Governance atrophy: The gradual degradation of a formally established governance structure into one that exists on paper but does not function in practice. Typically caused by inadequate operating model design rather than a lack of intent. The central risk addressed in Chapter 13.

Governance monitoring: The practice of tracking whether the institutional governance structures around AI systems remain current and effective: assessments on schedule, remediation tracked, inventory current, board briefings delivered. Distinct from performance and behavioral monitoring. See Chapter 11.

Inherent risk: The risk a system carries before any controls are applied, assessed based on classification level, data sensitivity, decision impact, and model opacity. The starting point of every AI risk assessment. See Chapter 5.

Information Security Program Manager (ISPM): The practitioner role that serves as the central protagonist throughout this book's scenarios and the primary owner of AI governance program activities at most credit unions. Used throughout the book to represent the security and risk practitioner who must build and operate a proportionate AI governance program.

Model opacity: The condition in which a vendor AI model's decision logic cannot be sufficiently explained by the vendor or understood by the institution to allow meaningful oversight. Creates an irreducible residual risk floor that controls alone cannot fully eliminate. See Chapters 5 and 6.

Model poisoning: An attack in which an adversary manipulates the data used to train an AI model, causing it to learn incorrect patterns or behave predictably under specific conditions that the attacker can later exploit. For credit unions consuming vendor AI, primarily a vendor-side threat. See Chapter 10.

Model transparency: One of the four AI Vendor Risk Evaluation Model categories. Addresses whether the institution can develop sufficient understanding of how a vendor's AI model functions to exercise meaningful oversight. The standard is functional transparency, not full disclosure. See Chapter 6.

NCUA (National Credit Union Administration): The federal agency that charters and supervises federal credit unions and insures member deposits at federally insured state-chartered credit unions. NCUA examiners apply AI governance expectations through existing technology and risk examination frameworks. Increasingly incorporating AI governance questions into safety and soundness examinations. See Chapter 3.

Operational dependence: One of the four AI Vendor Risk Evaluation Model categories. Addresses the risk that an institution's business processes become so reliant on a vendor's AI capabilities that a disruption—or gradual performance degradation—creates a material operational impact. See Chapters 6 and 11.

Performance monitoring: The ongoing practice of tracking whether an AI system is producing outputs consistent with its documented baseline. Requires a performance baseline established at deployment and institution-side outcome tracking in addition to vendor-provided metrics. See Chapter 11.

Prompt injection: An AI security attack in which malicious instructions are embedded in content that an AI system processes, causing it to produce outputs or take actions its operators did not intend. Most relevant for LLM-based member-facing applications such as chatbots and correspondence tools. See Chapter 10.

Proportionality: The regulatory standard against which AI governance programs are assessed: commensurate with the institution's size, complexity, and actual AI risk profile. Credit unions are not expected to operate enterprise AI governance infrastructure. They are expected to operate a defensible program appropriate to their environment. See Chapters 1, 2, and 12.

Residual risk: The risk that remains after controls have been applied to inherent risk. Expressed as the combination of inherent risk and control effectiveness. The metric that matters to leadership: how much risk the institution is actually carrying for a system today. See Chapter 5.

Risk appetite: A formal statement of the types and levels of risk the institution will accept in pursuit of its objectives. The board-level AI risk appetite statement establishes boundaries for AI deployment, data use, and transparency obligations. See Chapter 16.

Risk disposition: The institution's decision about what to do with assessed residual risk: accept, mitigate, transfer, avoid, or accept conditionally pending defined remediation actions with a specified timeline. Documented in the risk assessment record and reviewed by the Risk Committee. See Chapter 5.

Shadow AI: AI tools adopted by staff for use in their workflows without institutional awareness, approval, or governance review. Distinct from vendor-embedded AI because it arrives through individual human behavior rather than institutional procurement. Accumulates in high-productivity, high-data-sensitivity workflows. See Chapter 8.

SR 11-7: Supervisory Guidance on Model Risk Management, issued jointly by the Federal Reserve Board and the OCC in 2011. The most directly applicable regulatory framework for AI governance in financial services. Applies to any quantitative model used in decision-making, including machine learning models and AI-powered scoring systems. See Chapter 3.

Supply chain attack: An attack targeting the third-party components, libraries, or infrastructure on which an AI system depends, rather than attacking the institution's own systems directly. Affects all customers of a vendor platform simultaneously. Credit unions cannot audit vendor AI supply chains directly but can ask vendors about their software composition security practices. See Chapter 10.

UDAAP (Unfair, Deceptive, or Abusive Acts or Practices): A consumer protection standard enforced by the CFPB. Applies to AI-driven member-facing decisions that produce unfair or misleading outcomes, regardless of whether the outcome was intentionally discriminatory. Creates consumer protection exposure for AI used in lending, marketing, or account management. See Chapters 3 and 17.

Index

A

B

C

B. A. Salas, *AI Risk Management for Financial Institutions*,
https://doi.org/10.1007/979-8-8688-3353-3

I, J, K

L

M

N

T

U

V, W, X, Y, Z

GPSR Compliance
The European Union's (EU) General Product Safety Regulation (GPSR) is a set of rules that requires consumer products to be safe and our obligations to ensure this.

If you have any concerns about our products, you can contact us on

ProductSafety@springernature.com

In case Publisher is established outside the EU, the EU authorized representative is:

Springer Nature Customer Service Center GmbH
Europaplatz 3
69115 Heidelberg, Germany

www.ingramcontent.com/pod-product-compliance
Lightning Source LLC
LaVergne TN
LVHW050803061126
851857LV00012B/659
9798868833526